Keeping YOU on the Retirement Fairway

LIVE BETTER FROM TEE TO GREEN

Alfie Tounjian, CFP®

Advantage Retirement Group
FORT MYERS, FLORIDA

Alfie Tounjian/Advantage Retirement Group
8870 Daniels Pkwy
Fort Myers, FL 33912
www.advantageretirementgroup.com

Book layout ©2013 BookDesignTemplates.com

Keeping YOU on the Retirement Fairway/ Alfie Tounjian. —1st ed.
ISBN 978-1544870601

Contents

I would like to dedicate this book to my mom, Sandy Glass, who has always taught me right from wrong, and to always treat people with respect.

My mom, whom I love with all my heart, passed away in December 2016, just as we were finalizing this book.

Her death was a reminder of my life's calling ... to help others live the fullest retirements possible.

I realize my mom is still teaching me to do the right and righteous thing even after she is gone.

~Alfie Tounjian
Jan. 15, 2017

May 2016, the family's last Mother's Day together: (back from left) Alfie's son, Devon; Alfie; nephew, David; (front from left) mother, Sandy Glass; and wife, Tommie.

Foreword
by Cody Foster

In my role, I work every day with hundreds of independent financial advisors across the country. I see the critical and vital role they play in helping people like you enjoy a successful retirement. When it comes to success in your retirement, and frankly, your financial future, it's important to find someone you can trust, someone who believes in you and wants what is best for you. The author of this book, Alfie Tounjian, is that person. I know because he believed in me first.

A little over a decade ago, three college friends started a company called Advisors Excel with a vision of creating an organization that supported the best financial advisors in the country, putting them in a better position to help their clients enjoy retirement. We had big dreams, but just one problem: we were brand new. What successful advisor would be willing to bet on a couple of young kids trying to start and build their own business? It seemed like every advisor we talked to said the same thing, "NO THANKS."

Then one day, I had the chance to talk to one of the biggest advisors we had ever met. He had a thriving practice and had been super successful for decades. My palms were actually sweating the day of our scheduled phone call because I knew this was the kind of advisor we dreamed of working with, and deep down, I also knew we probably had no chance of convincing him to join us.

As we talked that day, I found out that not only was he a very successful advisor, but he had also hired and trained half a dozen other advisors. And as our conversation carried on, I was blown away by his kindness and his openness to giving us a chance. Before he would work with us, he said he wanted to meet us in person. He wanted to get to know us, understand who we were and what we stood for. So he invited us out to his office to meet him in person. This was a big step for us as a company … getting a chance to actually go meet an advisor who might work with us. Just when I thought things couldn't go any better, he did something totally unexpected. He opened his home to us and invited us to stay with him. That simple act of kindness led to what has become a decade-long friendship with one of the most genuine people I know, Alfie Tounjian.

It's fun, looking back over the past 11 years of our friendship. I've seen Alfie's son, Devon, grow from a 9-year-old boy into a young man. I've watched the example he's set in his marriage to Tommie, and I have tried to model his love in my own marriage. I've seen Alfie continue to train and help other advisors in our industry. I've seen him move back to his home state of Florida and start his business over from scratch, only to grow it into one of the most successful advisory practices in Southwest Florida. But more important than all of that, I've seen him take care of hundreds of his clients and do everything he can to help them build the retirements of their dreams.

Alfie's a student of the game, a real pro. He is always trying to learn new strategies and improve on the value he can provide his clients. He's a CERTIFIED FINANCIAL PLANNER™ professional, which shows his dedication to learning (only 20 percent of all financial advisors have earned a CFP® designation). Not only does he believe in educating himself, but he believes in educating his clients. Whether it's through his workshops, on his radio show, or through writing this book, he focuses on making sure his clients know the risks they'll face in retirement and how they can avoid them.

Despite his impressive resume, the thing I love most about Alfie is this: I know if I ever needed anything, he would be there for me and would do anything he could to help me. He's already done it once in a way he will never truly realize. I don't know about you, but that's the type of advisor, and person, I'd trust with my future. Come to think of it, in a way, I already did.

~Cody Foster
Co-founder, Advisors Excel
Topeka, Kansas
January 2017

Preface

saw a headline recently that stopped me in my tracks: "**10,000 Boomers Are Retiring Each Day.**"

That's a lot of people!

To put that in perspective, the football stadium where the Tampa Bay Buccaneers play is near where I work and live. It's one of the largest in the NFL. Packed to capacity, it holds almost 70,000 people. Imagine that many people retiring in the United States each week until around the year 2030!

According to the demographers who keep track of such things, the "retirement stampede" began in 2010. That's the year 10,000 baby boomers (those born between 1946 and 1964) began turning 65 every day. They refer to this as the "pig in the python" phenomenon. Because, when you look at a population timeline of the 20th century, the bulge in the birth rate after World War II is a rather sizeable bump in what is otherwise a steady trending chart.

What caused this sudden growth in the birth rate is obvious, of course. Soldiers came home after World War II, got married and started families. The country had also fought its way out of the Great Depression, and with America's newfound prosperity, the more-is-better seemed to apply to everything, including the size of the family.

No other generation in history has changed the world culturally and economically quite as much as the "boom" generation. It's hard to believe that the generation that brought us rock 'n' roll music, put a man on the moon, launched the hippie movement and coined the phrase, "Never trust anyone over 30" is now be-coming silver-haired retired folks.

Just as they revolutionized music, these baby boomers are in the process of redefining retirement. There was a time in America when you worked for the same employer for 25-30 years, received a gold watch, and started collecting a nice, fat pension. It's not that way anymore. Traditional pension plans are going the way of buffalo herds and polyester leisure suits. According to the Employee Benefit Research Institute, only 2 percent of American workers have a pension plan that guarantees them a steady lifetime income upon retirement.[1] Defined-*benefit* pension plans have been replaced with the invest-it-yourself defined-*contribution* plans. These days, you are fortunate if your employer matches a portion of what you contribute to these plans. The problem with 401(k)-type plans is they are usually based on the performance of the stock market. As anyone with a portfolio knows, the stock market has been on a roller coaster ride thus far in the 21st century. Wall Street watchers call the span from 2000 to 2010 the "lost decade." Why? Because, despite the frenetic activity of the market, when averaged out, the ups and downs resulted in little positive gain. Because retirement programs are no longer guaranteed, retirement security is jeopardized for millions of Americans.

Retirees also face other challenges these days. Some who were counting on the equity in their homes for support were hit hard when the housing bubble burst in 2007, and property values plummeted.

As a class, baby boomers have been good at spending and delinquent at saving. According to CBS Money Watch, "Baby boomers, those 55 to 65, said they want to have $45,500 in annual

---

[1] Employee Benefit Research Institute. 2014. "FAQs About Benefits – Retirement Issues." https://www.ebri.org/publications /benfaq/index.cfm?fa=retfaq14. Accessed Dec. 21, 2016.

retirement income, yet they've accumulated nest eggs that would generate only $9,150 annually, leaving a gap of $36,350."[2]

One of the challenges to retirement that wasn't there 50 to 75 years ago is that we are living longer these days. What's so bad about that? Nothing. That is, if you have enough money to last you your entire lifetime. But the fear we hear expressed most often from seniors is, what happens if I outlive my resources? Will I lose my independence? Will I become a burden to my family? It's a valid concern and one we will discuss in this book.

The Bottom Line

I want you, dear reader, to go into retirement *fully prepared* to meet these challenges. I would not want a family member or a close friend of mine entering retirement only to be ambushed by any of these challenges, so I do not wish it for you.

If you are retired, or if you are thinking about retiring in the next few years, and if you just don't have that warm and fuzzy feeling about the future that you feel you need, then you will find the contents of this book useful and reassuring. If you have a retirement plan, but just don't understand how it is working, then you will be interested in what we will discuss in the coming chapters.

When I first started hosting *"Saving the Investor,"* a financial TV and radio show that airs on several network channels in southwest Florida, I didn't realize just how concerned some retirees are about their financial future. For many of them, retirement is a new landscape with few guarantees and many challenges. When we talk about these important issues, even though I hold the CERTIFIED FINANCIAL PLANNER™ designation, I view my role as that of a coach more than an advisor. I enjoy educating people so they can

---

[2] Kate Gibson. CBS MoneyWatch. Oct. 22, 2015. "A yawning gap in baby boomers' retirement savings." http://www.cbsnews. com/news/gulf-in-needed-retirement-savings-for-baby-boomers/. Accessed Dec. 21, 2016

make informed choices and prudent decisions. I love to see the light bulb of understanding click on when we can use plain talk to enable listeners and viewers to grasp some of the financial issues they find baffling. Nothing brings me greater satisfaction than to receive a phone call or a letter from a viewer who says, "Thanks for clearing that up, Alfie! Now I understand."

I find that most of my listeners, viewers and readers want the same thing out of life: peace of mind and happiness. This book is written along the same lines as my TV and radio broadcasts. My objective is to simplify complex financial concepts, and to separate fact from fiction. It is necessary that we understand the choices we make with our wealth, just like we understand choices we make with our health. Can you imagine going to your doctor with a physical ailment, only to learn that he or she just wants to sell you pills, and is not really interested in your overall health? You expect a concerned physician to ask you lots of questions, and learn about your health history in full detail before prescribing a treatment plan. It should be the same in the financial advisory profession, but unfortunately this is not always the case.

In this book, we will discuss the difference between the "accumulation phase" of our financial lives and the "harvesting phase." When financial advisors don't know the difference, and advise their older clients using the same investing strategies as they do their younger clients, it can be a recipe for financial disaster.

What you will not find in this book is a get-rich-quick scheme, or a list of hot stock picks. This book is primarily about the money part of retirement, not what to do with the leisure time you have earned.

We may explore some new territory, and examine some fresh approaches to investing. So, please keep an open mind, and hear me out when we come to those. The retirement landscape is constantly changing. Keeping up with those changes is vital to financial success and Keeping YOU on the Retirement Fairway!

CHAPTER ONE

Finding Your Financial Purpose

I believe in purpose-driven finance. What does that phrase mean, exactly? Simply that money and wealth mean nothing without a purpose. They are just numbers on an account ledger, or figures and digits on a computer screen, if you don't have a purpose attached to them.

I could go on for pages and pages here about how to acquire, invest and preserve wealth, but it matters not if at the end of it all there is no purpose attached to its acquisition and preservation. And everyone's purpose is different. I saw a bumper sticker the other day that bore the somewhat cynical expression about wealth, "Whoever dies with the most toys wins." I thought about that little slogan as I pulled by the car in the passing lane. If that was all the significance one attached to wealth, just the fun and amusement that it could buy, then, yes, I suppose it would make the whole endeavor pointless and futile. But that's not the case for people who attach purpose and meaning to their wealth.

It makes me think of a story I once read about a man who stopped to watch men who were working on a great stone wall, appearing to be the beginning of a church of some sort. He asked one of the masons, "What are you doing?"

"I'm laying stone," snapped the man. "What does it look like I'm doing?" The worker was obviously out of sorts and not happy with his job.

The observer moved down the line and asked another mason, this one with a cheerful expression on his face, what he was doing.

"I'm building a cathedral that will provide a place for families to worship for centuries," he said, beaming with pride.

The point is, if you have a financial purpose in life, your outlook will be healthier. Your purpose could be no more complicated than caring for your family. Just seeing to it that your spouse and children have a comfortable home and a good education could be purpose enough. You could have goals that include personal enrichment through travel. Altruistic endeavors, such as charitable contributions or public service, could be your aim. Or it could be that you wish to safeguard your personal security during retirement, and whatever is left over, you wish to leave to future generations as a legacy.

I had to smile at another bumper sticker I saw on the back of a motor home one day. It was partially covered with the tire of a trail bike someone had lashed to the stern of the road behemoth, so I had to crane my neck as I passed to make it out. It read: "We are spending our children's inheritance." I'm sure there was a story there, and a reason why they saw fit to install that particular slogan on the bumper. At least you can't say they didn't have a goal!

Finding Your Purpose

To find your financial purpose, you have to decide what matters to you most. That may sound simple, but for some it is like the $64,000 question. What do I *really* want to accomplish with my wealth? When you look past the basics of food, clothing and shelter, what else is on the list? Security? Personal growth as a human being? Peace of mind? The truth is, only you can decide.

One person might think owning a home in the mountains and one at the beach is the ultimate goal, while another is satisfied with rather modest living quarters, but will not rest until he sees his or her grandchildren successful in life. It depends on the individual.

But be assured that your purpose for money, once you establish it, is both your source of motivation and your rudder. It will guide you when it comes to investing, saving, making charitable donations and especially spending, for the rest of your life.

An exercise I recommend is to get a pad and pencil and try to write out in one or two sentences what your financial purpose is. Sort of like corporations do mission statements. At least it will make you think. What DO I want to do in my financial life? While you are there, write out five distinct long-range goals. It is important to be specific here. And since we are dealing with money here, put a dollar sign to them when appropriate.

MY FINANCIAL PURPOSE

What are my values and passions? _____

_____

_____

_____

What do I want to do in my financial life? _____

_____

_____

_____

My financial purpose is: _____

_____

_____

_____

My five long-range financial goals are:

1._____

2._____

3._____

4._____

5._____

For example:

MY FINANCIAL PURPOSE: "To ensure that my children are sufficiently educated to begin their secular careers in life, and then to guarantee my spouse and I have a secure income stream that will allow us to remain independent for the rest of our lives and not become a burden on our loved ones. The remainder I will leave as a legacy to help my unborn grandchildren, with 10 percent for my church."

FIVE LONG-RANGE FINANCIAL GOALS

1. Create $100,000 annual income in retirement
2. Retire in 4 years
3. Pay cash for new car in next 12 months
4. Pledge $1,000 to Orphans Hospital in next 12 months
5. Finish installing cedar sauna in old utility room by January

Those were just thrown out there as examples. Your goals will be unique to you because YOU are unique to you and your family. But the key is to be specific. Without specificity, goals are merely wishes. "Retire comfortably" is a wish. "Retire in four years with $100,000 guaranteed income" is meaningful. Why? Because it has the teeth of specificity.

Going over one young couple's goals, the wife blurted: "Make a million dollars!" when asked about their income goals. Then she laughed, and so did the husband. I chuckled, but thought to myself, "These are bright, young people – well educated and full of promise. They could do that if they believed it. But, because they didn't, it would likely never happen. They were selling themselves short, but they seemed to be very happy, which was worth more than the million dollars, in my estimation.

Remember, money is merely currency. It is an *instrument* to reach the real goal; it is not the *true* goal. People assume that we reach financial goals by investing and managing those investments. But the real path to goal achievement starts with your values, your passions and your thought processes. A good financial "coach" coaxes out those feelings and helps you identify them, thereby helping you create and identify goals. The next step is to put in place and quantify the objectives that are stepping stones to those goals.

Having $1 million is not a personal value, it is a quantifiable objective. The value is independence, or security. The money helps us fulfill the value. It's the passion for the value that motivates and steers us.

Money does not buy happiness, it's true. But it can provide us with choices and afford us the time and opportunity to fulfill our values. Like author and motivational Zig Ziglar said, "Money isn't the most important thing in life, but it's reasonably close to oxygen on the 'gotta have it' scale."

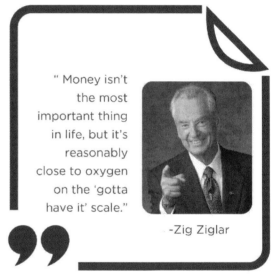

" Money isn't the most important thing in life, but it's reasonably close to oxygen on the 'gotta have it' scale."

-Zig Ziglar

Once you've determined your financial purpose, you have the goal in mind. Metaphorically, you've stepped onto the tee box and are looking down the retirement fairway. It's time to take your stance, set your eyes on the target, and avoid the potential hazards that lurk in the rough.

Finding My Purpose of Money

Money was always tight when I was growing up. We never went hungry, and we always had a warm, dry place to sleep, but there was precious little extra to go around. Money – or should I say the lack of an abundant supply of it – was always a topic of conversation in our house.

It was perhaps because of this that I formed a goal early in my life. I was determined to earn a good income when I became an adult. I vowed to myself that when I eventually married and had a family of my own, I would provide well for them, and lack of money would not be a problem. Call it the exuberance of youth, but I knew beyond a shadow of a doubt that I could accomplish my goal. And, through hard work and perseverance, I did. Later in life, I would care well for my wife and family, and help provide a more comfortable life for my mother as well. My wife, Tommie, and I were able to provide a nice home and a good education for our son. So, financially, I did what I set out to do – or so I thought.

I was a church-goer as a youth. As young parents, Tommie and I regularly went to church. When we moved to Fort Myers, we started attending a new church where we liked the teaching we received there each week from "Pastor Matt." His messages challenged us to grow. One Sunday, the pastor was talking about tithing, the practice of donating a tenth of one's income to the church.

At first, I thought, "Oh, brother! Here we go again – another sermon on money." But as I sat there, something tugged at my heart and started making sense to me. I finally understood that what I thought was my money was really God's money, and that He had given it to me to use. I was merely a steward of it. I began to realize that my owning my own business was a blessing from God, and that I didn't earn it all by myself. God had equipped me with the ability to help other people, and the income that followed was merely a product of that gift. My thinking went deeper. "If all belongs to God, then why am I keeping it all to myself?"

When Pastor Matt challenged us with the idea of contributing 10 percent of our income to the church, I thought, "Wow! How could I possibly give up 10 percent?" We were in the habit of giving a little here and there, and maybe a little extra at Christmas, but I couldn't imagine giving 10 percent of what I made throughout the year. That was just over the top!

Tommie and I had a quiet drive home that day. We were both mulling over what the pastor had said. During lunch, we started talking about tithing and it became a deep conversation. What was the purpose of our money, anyway? We decided to take Pastor Matt's challenge seriously and commit to tithing. In doing so, we found a new purpose for our money. It was not just to fatten our wallets, but to give back to God a portion of that with which he had already blessed us.

Later, I remember overhearing Tommie talking excitedly to one of our staff members. "We want to make more so we can give more!"

What a pendulum shift! When I was young, I did not want to live an uncomfortable life. I also had a strong desire to build a successful business so I could care for my family and my mother. Those remain a priority, but now money means a great deal more to us. When we realized that what we have is a gift from God, tithing and generosity became a way of life for us.

This discovery has extended into our business life as well. We now have a culture of generosity at our office. We are constantly looking for ways to bless other people, whether with a simple note of encouragement, or taking food to someone who is sick, or helping out in a ministry that provides food for the less fortunate people in our community.

I only tell you this story because it's true. At one time, I was worried that I would not have enough and I didn't want to go without. Now, I feel so blessed that I have discovered the real purpose for money.

One of the first questions I ask people when I sit down with them is, "What is your purpose for money?" It is a question that only you can answer, and your answer will be unique to you.

Imagine you and I are on the golf course together. You step onto the first tee box. What do you do? You gaze down the fairway and look for the pin. That's your objective. You want to use your mental concentration, your skill and imagination to put the ball into the 4.25-inch diameter hole at the bottom of that flag. I am your caddy, your golf coach. I have played on this course and studied it carefully. I want to keep you on the fairway and out of the rough so you can realize your true purpose for your money.

CHAPTER TWO

Avoiding the Hazards

Those who know me well know I play a little golf from time to time, as the title and cover of this book suggest. When people ask, "How do you shoot?" I know they want a numerical answer, but I usually dodge the question and say, "Not too bad today, but I'm getting better." The truth is – and most people who love the sport feel this way – I am never quite satisfied with my score. I want it to be better, which is why I take advantage of any good coaching I can get.

Golf is a demanding game. Not physically so much, although it does require a certain degree of physical stamina, but psychologically. The pros make it look easy when you watch them play, but trust me on this. They may make it *look* easy, but what you don't see are the hours of practice they put into the game. They constantly work on the small things, like stance, swing, club selection and grip. What you see when they play represents countless hours of instruction and practice.

What impresses me with the professional golfers I have met is that, no matter how successful they are, they still hire and listen to their coaches. They know better than to take their innate skills for granted. They recognize that one slip in concentration can cause them to miss that crucial putt, or send their ball into a hazard, costing them a championship or causing them to miss the cut. The best pros will show up on the Thursday morning before a weekend tournament and quietly begin practicing. You may even see them practicing their swing accompanied by a coach with a video camera. The coach is recording and scrutinizing their swing. The coach's job is not to play the game *for* the pros, but to guide them, and help them hone their skills.

I am a *financial* coach. My job is to help people who want to win the game of retirement make the right choices and, *stay in the fairway*, so to speak. I can't resist the golf metaphors, because retirement is like golf in many ways. You only get one shot at retirement. No mulligans are allowed. And it is so easy to goof it up if you aren't careful.

As on any well-designed golf course, there are many hazards to retirement. I work and live in the Fort Myers/Naples area of Florida, a sun-drenched state that is home to more than 1,100 public and private golf courses. At least 70 of them are located in the Fort

Myers/Naples area. One of the most scenic and toughest of these is Old Corkscrew Golf Club, a private course designed by Jack Nicklaus. It's beautiful to look at, but challenging to play. Mr. Nicklaus saw to it that you have plenty of water hazards and sand traps for your ball to plop into. And try to keep your ball out of the Palmettos if you can. One of the best pieces of advice ever given by one golfer to someone wishing to play this course was: "Play this one with someone who knows the course, if you can."

As I said, my job as a financial coach is to keep you out of the retirement hazards. What might those be?

Running Out of Income

The baby boomer generation is living longer than any other generation that has ever lived. That is a good thing *if* you have enough money to last throughout your retirement.

When I meet with people in our Fort Myers or Naples offices, I am often asked the question, "How much money will I need to retire?" That's a good question. No one knows exactly how long he or she is going to live on this earth. But I know plenty of people personally who are still going strong at age 90-plus. They say 60 is the new 40, and there are lots of personal friends of mine who make me believe that is true!

More and more senior citizens are spending 30 years or longer in retirement. Having the financial means to fund that period in their lives is crucial. People shudder at the thought of getting to a certain age, and running out of personal resources, losing their independence, becoming a burden on their loved ones, or becoming a ward of the state. The real questions are: "Is there a way to keep my independence and self-determination as long as I am alive?" And, "Is there a way to use what I have now to guarantee an income to fund my financial future?" The answer to both of those is "maybe." Keep reading. We will get to that later on. But running out of money is one of those traps waiting for you on the back nine and there may be ways to play around it, as we shall see.

Failing to Plan

No one – at least no one I know of – consciously plans to fail. That would be contrary to logic and human nature, wouldn't it? But the woods are full of people who fail to plan. It has even become proverbial: "People don't plan to fail – they just fail to plan." Why is that? For some, it is because they are intimidated by all the choices they have to make. Take Social Security decisions for example. Most people are eligible to take their Social Security at age 62. But should they? Or, should they wait until age 66, which is what the Social Security Administration calls the full retirement age for most folks today? Or, should they postpone it until age 70?

Decisions associated with planning can be intimidating. It's like the person who once got a job sorting bad oranges off a conveyer belt. Someone one asked him how he liked his job.

"It's OK except for the pressure," he responded.

"Pressure? What pressure? All you do is toss bad oranges off a conveyer belt!"

"I know," he said. "But all day long, it's nothing but decisions, decisions, decisions!"

We may feel that way without a guide. A "coach" to help us. We will get to that, too. So just stay tuned.

Paralysis Through Analysis

That's another trap I like to help people play around when they are entering the retirement zone – over-analyzing things. This syndrome is the exact opposite of ignoring the problem. Unlike those who ignore the problem, the over-analyzers wind up thinking about it so much they can't make a decision. The expression for that is "paralysis through analysis." Everybody will have between five and eight really great opportunities in life, but many fail to take advantage of them because they just aren't sure they have collected enough data.

This is especially true when it comes to investing. To use a golfing metaphor, in tournament play, the closer you get to the clubhouse, the more critical your strokes become. You have fewer holes to make up for what happened behind you. This can cause some people to lose their confidence. Or you may be going in with your best score ever, and you start to think things like: "Don't mess up. Avoid the water," and you start playing not to lose instead of playing to win.

During your working years, when most of the sand is in the top half of your hourglass, you are bolder with your investment decisions, and this is altogether appropriate. You are still in the accumulation phase of your financial life. Time is on your side. Once you retire and cut the umbilical paycheck cord, you are dealing with what essentially becomes a nonrenewable resource. So playing it *safer* should be your watchword. But you can become so careful that you don't allow your money to work for you. In helping you avoid this hazard, my job as your financial coach is to show you ways you can retire with confidence – knowing for certain that your assets are prudently allocated.

If you are an analyzer, you will need not hollow promises, but *proof* based on accurate information, that your finances are properly positioned. You need to be comfortable with this knowledge, just the way you know your right shoe is on your right foot and your left shoe is on your left foot. Investing and preparing for retirement can be somewhat complex, but a good financial coach should be able to take the mystery out of all of it for you. You may be surprised, as you continue reading, at how many strategies and financial tools are available to you these days if you are entering retirement.

A good financial coach will also listen and observe with the goal of custom-fitting all counsel, advice and recommendations to your unique financial situation and goals. A good golf coach will understand the playing conditions of the day. My job is to know and understand the environment in which you will be investing and saving for your retirement. The economy and the financial landscape are constantly changing. Changing with it is necessary if your portfolio is to thrive. A financial coach helps folks understand how the market works and the truth about investing, so their movements will be sure-footed and they will be confident of the ground on which they are standing financially.

"Retire with confidence" is a recurring theme you will read in my firm's literature and on the company's website, http://savingtheinvestor.com. Confidence is an ethereal quality of the mind and heart. Confidence is an emotion, true, but not a baseless one. When it comes to investing, the foundation of confidence is understanding. I promise you I will make sure you understand how the market works, the truth about investing and how to be a prudent investor.

Investing Emotionally

Here's a hazard that trips up many a retiree – trying to time the stock market by looking for that next Google or Apple stock; landing the big one, as they say. Chapter 3 in this book will deal with this. Look for it later on, as we present scientific evidence that helps dispel the myth that it is possible to predict precisely what any market will do (and it *is* a myth, despite the insistence and repetitions of some financial advisors). We will discuss the emotions of investing and how to work around falling victim to them.

"But wait a minute, Alfie," I can hear someone out there say. "What about those mutual fund managers who have five-star ratings? Aren't they possessed with special knowledge beyond what is normal? Aren't they blessed with IQs so high they can just know which way the market will move before the opening bell?" Well – and I'm sorry to be the one to burst this bubble if you believe in this fairy tale, but – the short answer is no. They can't, they aren't and they don't. But keep reading. We will get to that, and how the mutual fund rating system works, and what investors need to be on the lookout for in that regard.

DO-IT-YOURSELF?

Are you a do-it-yourselfer? On some things, I am. And it has backfired on me occasionally. Recently, when a toilet began leaking at our house, my wife, Tommie, asked me to call a plumber. From somewhere deep within me, an urge to fix it myself came to the fore. "I can handle it," I said with a note of self-confidence. "Let me take a look."

The leak appeared to be coming from the tank above the toilet bowl. Determined to find its source, I sat on the toilet seat, facing the tank and started my investigation by removing the tank lid. I put the ceramic lid on my lap and asked Tommie to roll up my sleeves so I could put my hands into the water and feel around for whatever was loose. But everything seemed to be tight.

With my wet hands, I grasped the lid to put it back on the tank. This is where things went bad. The tank lid slipped out of my hands and came crashing down on the top of the tank, cracking the ceramic. Now, water was rushing all over the floor. "Grab a bucket," I yelled, quickly flushing the toilet to slow the flood. I finally found the valve and turned off the water supply, and stood up to survey the damage.

Needless to say, we had to replace the whole toilet, and what was once a $100 plumber's repair job had now become a $600 lesson on why it is sometimes wise to leave it to the professionals.

Long-Term-Care Costs

The cost of long-term care is the "elephant in the room"; many people just don't want to talk about, but it is there. There is a chance you will someday need home health care, assisted living or nursing home care. It may be stating the obvious, but ignoring a threat is not a good way of dealing with it.

"Isn't that covered under Medicare?"

The short answer is no. Ordinary health insurance doesn't cover it either. And covering the cost of long-term care can rob you of your life's savings.

Some folks change the subject on this one because the only solution they know about is traditional long-term-care insurance and they usually don't start thinking about purchasing it until it becomes prohibitively expensive. We will present some alternative solutions in this book you may find interesting. Of course, the best way to avoid this eventuality is to stay healthy, live a good, long life and die with your boots on. However, according to statistics, the chances of needing some type of long-term health care are as follows: Someone turning age 65 today has almost a **70 percent** chance of needing some type of long-term-care services and support in their remaining years. Women typically need care longer (3.7 years) than men (2.2 years). One-third of today's 65 year-olds may never need long-term care support, but **20 percent** will need it for longer than five years.[3]

So, we need to talk about the "elephant in the room" from a standpoint of what you can *feasibly* do to keep that ominous hazard from destroying your nest egg and financially wrecking your retirement.

---

[3] U.S. Department of Health and Human Services. "How Much Care Will You Need?" http://longtermcare.gov/the-basics/how-much-care-will-you-need. Accessed Dec. 22, 2016.

Sequence of Returns Trap

If you haven't heard of this one, we need to talk. It can be a monster. It is responsible for eating up more retirement assets than the lake on the 18th hole eats golf balls, especially for those who aren't paying attention to where their assets are positioned *when they enter retirement.* Particularly vulnerable to this hazard are those who believe in the myth of the so-called "4 percent rule" of investing. We will climb into that in more detail later, but this is one you need to avoid at all costs.

False Diversification

One of the biggest lies ever told to investors goes like this:
"Are our invested assets fully protected?"
"Yes, they are, Mr. and Mrs. Investor. You see, they are *fully diversified.*"
Don't get me wrong. True diversification is a good thing – a great thing. The problem is that some investors *think* they are diversified when they are not. We will get into what true diversification is and what it is not and how you can tell the difference. We will explain why you want a portfolio that does not rely on market timing, track record investing and stock picking, but does reflect true diversification and asset classes, and where returns come from.

Bad Advice

There's only one thing worse than not having advice on a challenging golf course, and that's having bad advice. If you have watched a major tournament on TV you have probably noticed the pro will, from time to time, confer with his caddie before a shot. What are they talking about? And why would the guy who carries the pro's bags be so highly paid? Some professional caddies make six figures, because they do much more than carry the clubs around. They are more like the second member of a two-person team. The caddie often keeps track of distance so the pro can select the right club. Professional golf has some pretty quirky rules, too. Yet, if they are not strictly adhered to, it can cost the pro the game. Surprisingly, many pros don't understand all the little nuances of the rule book and what provisions are and are not available to them when they are in trouble. A good caddie will know that stuff, and be able to advise his "boss."

Many a game has been won because of good advice from a proficient, well-trained caddie, or lost because of lack of same.

We have a chapter on getting good financial advice and how you can know if the advice you are following is the best for your individual situation. When it comes to financial planning and avoiding the hazards of retirement, no two individuals are alike. That is why there should be no cookie-cutter plans out there, but you would be surprised at how many people either have no plan, or are following a financial strategy designed for the masses and not them as individuals.

CHAPTER THREE

Planning for 85 and Beyond

ell, I have good news and I have bad news.

What's the good news?

People are living longer!

What's the bad news?

People are living longer!

I don't get it, Alfie! What could possibly be bad about living longer?

As I said before, nothing, if you are prepared for it financially.

I saw two surveys recently, one by Allianz Insurance Company of North America and another by Wells Fargo, that revealed the same statistic. The one thing that seniors fear the most – more than death, even – is running out of money. Is it a legitimate concern? Absolutely![4, 5]

---

[4] Neil Dwane. Allianz Global Investors. June 8, 2016. "Living Longer: An Expensive Curse?" http://us.allianzgi.com/Commen tary/MarketInsights/Pages/is-living-longer-an-expensive-curse.aspx. Accessed Dec. 22, 2016.

[5] Wells Fargo Investment Institute. 2016. "Living Longer, Living Better." https://investmentinstitute.wf.com/living-longer-retirement-planning/#footer-alternative-investments. Accessed Dec. 22, 2016.

Living How Much Longer?

If you make it to 65, the Social Security Administration predicts you can expect to live to at least age 84 if you are of average health. That's for men. Women can tack on a couple of extra years. Keep in mind, those are **averages.** One out of every four 65-year-olds today will live past age 90, SSA statistics tell us, and one out of 10 will live past age 95![6] The way life expectancy works, the longer you **have** lived, the longer you probably **will** live. Back in 1900, the average male life expectancy was only 46! When President Franklin D. Roosevelt signed the Social Security Act of 1935, life expectancy had gone up to 63. So what are the chances of you spending 20, even 30 or more years in retirement? Pretty good, actually.

No Help from Wall Street

During the decade of the 1990s, some investors didn't worry one whit about retirement, because they figured that Wall Street would just keep pumping out profits for the rest of their lives. They could park their assets in those gleaming glass and steel tower canyons of the financial district and coast through life without a care, collecting their gains from an unending fountain of money. We all know what happened to that dream – the decade of the 2000s came along. The word volatile just doesn't describe it; it was Mr. Toad's wild ride!

Some call what transpired in the decade of the 2000s the "curse of the good times." In the 1990s, everything you touched in the stock market seemed to turn to gold. In those days, all you had to do was take the mutual fund page out of the Wall Street Journal, paste it to the wall, and throw a dart at it. Invest your money wherever the point of the dart hit, and you could realize a 20–30

---

[6] Social Security Administration. 2016. "Calculators: Life Expectancy." https://www.ssa.gov/planners/lifeexpectancy.html. Accessed Dec. 22, 2016.

percent gain. If you think I'm exaggerating, a story appeared in several national newspapers in 1999 describing an experiment involving a 6-year-old chimpanzee by the name of Raven who put on a show for the press by tossing darts at a list of 133 internet companies taped to the wall. Wall Street was riding the technology wave at the time, and the chimp couldn't miss. As it turns out, the little primate outdid human fund managers! If she had been a real fund manager, her selections would have been ranked as the 22nd best in the country out of 6,000 competitors.

In hindsight, it is easy to see the dot-com bubble for what it was. It was the Hindenburg coming in for a landing at Lakehurst, New Jersey – about to go down in flames. But not back then. It was a shock to millions of investors when, from March 11, 2000, to Oct. 9, 2002, the Nasdaq Composite lost 78 percent of its value, plunging from 5046.86 to 1114.11. In Silicon Valley, stunned overnight millionaires were fire-selling their $4 million mansions and moving back in with their parents.[7] What happened next? The economy temporarily recovered. One of the strongest housing booms in America's history ensued. By 2005, the staccato sound of hammers could be heard rattling the air in the outskirts of American cities, especially in the sunbelt states. Bankers were whistling "Happy Days Are Here Again." The Federal Reserve was cooperating nicely by keeping interest rates at an all-time low. If you could fog a mirror in those days, you could borrow money to buy a house. Then what happened? In 2007, the housing bubble burst. Mortgage-backed securities plunged. Banks that were "too big to fail" had to be bailed out by Uncle Sam. Home values plunged. Foreclosure signs started popping up in front lawns like dandelions after a spring rain. On Sept. 29, 2008, the Dow fell 777.68 points – the most in any single day in history and the Dow

---

[7] Andrew Beattie. Investopedia. "Market Crashes: The Dotcom Crash." http://www.investopedia.com/features/crashes/crashes 8.asp. Accessed Dec. 22, 2016.

Jones Industrial Average, long regarded as the barometer of the economy plunged to a new low, losing half its value.[8]

Some market analysts have called the decade from 2000 to 2010 the "lost decade." There was plenty of action alright, but little accomplishment. The market surged up and then plunged back down, ultimately leaving investors right back where they started.

Too many investors continued to invest in the 21st century the same way they did in the 20th century. That was why millions of retiring Americans lost as much as half their life's savings in the 2008 market crash. It didn't have to be like that! In fact, it wasn't like that for a lot of people I know. The "modern portfolios" I use faired really well during those times because of aggressive rebalancing, owning different asset classes along with being invested in over 45 countries. Remember, returns come from owning the market.

Emotions and Investing

Emotions have a way of robbing investors of the nest eggs they need for retirement. I can only imagine how many worried investors called their financial advisors looking for explanations and hope.

"Hello, Mr. Advisor? This is Janet Smith. I'm 58 years old and I entrusted you with all of my money. I'm losing a ton of it, and I am scared. What should I do?"

"Oh, Ms. Smith, don't you know that the stock market always comes back?"

Was that financial advisor lying? No. The market *does* always come back. What the advisor couldn't tell her, however, was *when.* She might have to live to be 115 before she gets back to even.

---

[8] Paul Kosakowski. Investopedia. "The Fall of the Market in the Fall of 2008." http://www.investopedia.com/articles/economics/ 09/subprime-market-2008.asp. Accessed Dec. 22, 2016.

As I write this book, there are some great financial minds out there who think that we are in for a long stretch of ups and downs that will average out to even. A sideways market, in other words. As I see it, my job is to remove the question marks and provide solutions.

How do we take the emotion out of investing? We will have a chapter later in this book that goes into more detail on this, but in brief we start by exposing what is in the investor's portfolio by doing what I call a "Financial MRI."

In medical parlance, an MRI (magnetic resonance imaging) scan uses radio waves and strong magnetic impulses to create pictures on a computer of tissue that an X-ray machine wouldn't pick up. Such detailed pictures can detect a tumor, for example, in someone complaining of persistent pain, such as a headache. It has been a real life-saver for many.

The Financial MRI examines the portfolio the same way – exposing hidden fees investors may have no idea they are paying. It will show them their true returns versus what they thought they were getting. It will also expose how diversified they are versus how diversified they may have *thought* their portfolio to be. Most of all, it will show whether the investor may be taking undue risk for the returns they are getting.

What comes next is crucial. When investors *are* taking undue risk, we show them how to *reduce* the risk and how it may be possible to keep their returns the same, or in some cases, even increase them.

Allocation, Allocation, Allocation

If you are buying a home for the purposes of resale, or starting up a retail business, the key is location, location, location. They key to a portfolio's performance is allocation, allocation, allocation. One study looked at the decade from 1977 to 1987 and delved into the particulars of more than 80 investment plans and found that 91.5 percent of the results were directly attributable to the investment allocations.[9] Think of allocations as a football team. Instead of individual players running their own plays, the team is working together, giving them the best opportunity to win the game.

For example, I've been a Miami Dolphins football fan for my whole life, but the New England Patriots have dominated the NFL for the past decade. Their head coach, Bill Belichick, is a master at bringing out the best in his players. He puts them in the proper positions to make plays as a team, ultimately giving them a better chance of winning the game. The same goes for a portfolio. With a "team" of asset classes working together, a portfolio has the best opportunity for return with the least amount of risk.

Staying Retired

The days of the pension are all but gone. If you have one, consider yourself lucky. But does that negate the need for a lifetime guaranteed income? Absolutely not. Because retirees may spend multiple decades in retirement, it is more crucial than ever that they have an income plan, knowing they will have enough money to last them through their retirements. Not just any income plan, but one that guarantees (not projects) an income stream for as long as they live. If they are a couple, then "as long as they *both* shall live."

And it should be in writing. In other words, the guarantee should be locked down and rock solid.

---

[9] Gary P. Brinson, Gilbert L. Beebower, Brian D. Singer. Financial Analysts Journal. May/June 1991. "Determinants of Portfolio Performance II: An Update." Vol. 47, Iss. 3. http://www. cfapubs.org/doi/pdf/10.2469/faj.v47.n3.40. Accessed Dec. 22, 2016.

What a shame it is for someone to work 40 years, then retire, and 10 years later have to go back to work again just to meet expenses. And yet it happens to those who don't prepare well.

Don't get me wrong. If you **want** to work after you retire, that's your business. In fact, I know of many who have rewarding second careers doing what they love. No, what I'm talking about is being **forced** back into the workplace because you simply ran out of resources and had to seek employment. As I say over and over on my radio and TV shows, that's no way to spend your golden years, folks.

So the two cornerstones to planning for financial independence for age 85 and beyond are:

A. Comprehensive Financial MRI

B. Comprehensive Lifetime Income Plan

Bottom line, now that we are living longer, we have to be wiser with our investing and saving choices. Russ Wiles, financial writer for the *Arizona Republic*, put it best: "The affordability part of living longer will require people to become more disciplined, improve their financial literacy and embrace assets, from stock funds to annuities, with which they might not have high comfort or familiarity. In some cases, it also will involve an adjustment in attitudes and behaviors."

Stanford Center on Longevity board member Russell Hill says that young people should save 15 percent of their income and older individuals will need "the lifelong income provided by annuities as well as professional money-management help."

Wiles continued: "If life spans lengthen, more people will want to enhance their knowledge of financial basics — the high costs of debt, the importance of stocks and other growth assets, the long-term impact of compounding and so on."

I totally agree.

Financial Phases

The two financial phases of life are:

- Accumulation
- Harvesting

Just as we go through physical stages in life, we advance through financial stages as well. When you are in your younger working years, you are in what I call the "accumulation" phase of your financial life. You are working, saving, investing, living life, maybe starting a family, buying homes and cars, and doing all the other things that go along with the American dream. Generally speaking, investors are more aggressive with their investing during the accumulation phase.

Have you ever heard of the Rule of 100? It is an investing rule of thumb. Take your age and subtract it from 100. That's the highest percentage of your investible assets you may want to consider having at risk. According to this "rule," the rest should be safe from market loss.

What does that suggest for someone in their 30s or 40s? They should have most of their assets aggressively invested for growth. Why might that be appropriate? Because time is on their side. They have time to wait for a stock market to recover after a correction. When you invest systematically each month, you are dollar-cost averaging – buying as values go up and down.

When someone is approaching retirement, however, we feel they should be more cautious. You enter the harvesting phase of your financial life, when it is arguably more important for you to keep what you have than to take excessive risk to accumulate more.

The harvesting phase comes when you are no longer receiving a paycheck and must depend completely on what you have accumulated and the interest you are able to obtain from those assets. Consider that a nonrenewable resource – not to be wasted or put under the unnecessary strain of excessive risk. Not if you want to make your money last as long as you do.

My 1990s Roller Coaster Ride

It was 1998, and life was good. Tommie and I were growing our insurance business in Maryland and we enjoyed traveling to new places and making new friends. One of our good friends was Mike from Atlanta. Mike traveled quite a bit too, and he often came to Florida on business. We enjoyed many conversations over dinner, and I admired Mike for his good business sense.

During one of these conversations, Mike told me about "Edith," his stockbroker in New York City, who, in his words, "wasn't your typical broker." He said that she could get me in on the ground floor with new private companies just as they were seeking capital to expand and launching their initial public offerings (IPOs).

"She has made me a lot of money," Mike told me. "I will try to see if she will take you on as a client."

I subsequently spoke to Edith and learned that she was associated with a large New York brokerage firm. I must confess, I liked what she told me.

"We will invest your money in tech stocks that have high potential for growth," she said.

She did warn me that I could lose some money, but she spent a lot more time telling me how much I could make. I decided to give her a try. I gave her $50,000 to work with. Within four or five months, the $50,000 became $100,000. So, I did what anyone else would do. I gave her another chunk of money – $200,000 this time. That was a lot of money for me to invest, but I wasn't thinking about what I could lose. I was thinking about how much I could gain.

Within two years, my original investment of $250,000 grew to $763,000. I couldn't have been more pleased.

In 2000, my wife, Tommie, and I, along with our son, Devon, went on a one-week cruise to the Caribbean. We were having a great time until I happened to catch the news and saw what was happening in the stock market. My wonderful vacation suddenly turned into one of the worst weeks I can remember. The market was falling harder and harder each day. There was no communication available. I couldn't call Edith to find out what was going on with my investments until I returned to the United States.

When we returned home, the first thing I did was look at my account. I was devastated. We had lost more than $300,000 of that $763,000. I tried desperately to contact Edith, but she was repeatedly "unavailable." The only person I could get through to was her assistant.

"Don't worry, Mr. Tounjian," she said. "It will come back. Just ride it out. It is a five-year plan." I told her I didn't like this five-year plan very much.

I never got a return call from Edith. Meanwhile, I continued to "ride it out," hoping that, if I waited, my investment would come back, as Edith's assistant had promised. Painfully, I watched as my hard-earned money continued to evaporate like smoke in the wind. "What goes up must come down, and what comes down must go up," I kept telling myself, as I waited for a reversal in the market that never came. Finally, my $736,000 had eroded to $63,000. My emotions were running wild! All I had wanted to do was grow my money, but I didn't sign up for this! Needless to say, working with a stockbroker and being exposed to so much risk had lost its appeal. I finally reached a point where I was so sick and tired of watching the market and seeing my investment evaporate that I said, "Enough is enough – cash me out!"

That was a defining moment for me. I knew that if I felt this way, there must be others out there who were sick and tired of this kind of emotional roller coaster ride with their hard-earned money. I wanted to do something about it.

Unlike myself, the vast majority of my clients were in retirement, or nearing retirement, and they didn't have the time to make up their losses in the market. I decided to build a practice that could help people invest for the long term, and develop strategies for them that would ensure they would never be put in the position that I was in. I became a Registered Financial Consultant and CFP® professional. I now had the tools and skills to help those who had trusted me, not only with their insurance needs, but also with the money from which they needed long-term growth.

My story resonates with many people who walk through the front door of our office for the first time. Each of them has a unique story of their own, sometimes more painful than mine, of taking on too much risk and not having a plan in place.

Volatility is inevitable, but taking on undue risk is avoidable.

CHAPTER FOUR

Taking the Emotion out of Investing

How can emotions betray investors? An age-old axiom of investors is "buy low and sell high." That's logical (and profitable) of course, but it often seems to be the reverse of what happens. Why? Because emotions get in the way.

To illustrate the point, I love the chart below from Philo Capital, an Australian investment firm. It says it all.

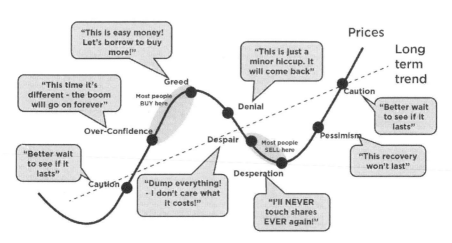

Isn't that exactly what happens? We want to buy low and sell high, but our emotions get in the way and we do the exact opposite.

DALBAR Inc. is a research organization that specializes in studying and measuring the behavior of investors – why they make the decisions they do. Each year they produce a report entitled "DALBAR's Quantitative Analysis of Investor Behavior." And each year the report reveals the average investor that does their own managing earns far less than professional investors for the very reasons suggested by the illustration above – emotional involvement.

To get a broad view of how the market is performing, all you have to do is look at a market index. The S&P (Standard & Poor's) 500, for example, takes 500 of the nation's largest companies and tracks the performance of their shares on the market. If an investor were to park money in an index fund and leave it there, his or her gains would mirror the performance of that index.

DALBAR's findings indicate that investors fall into the trap of trying to beat the index, however, and "time the market." There are several reasons they don't succeed. One is because it is impossible to time the market. I always say, if you are trying to time the market, you have to be right TWICE! You have to know when to get in and when to get out and keep repeating it over and over – a very hard thing to do.

Another reason is because investors tend to lead with their emotions. Even if we could invest without emotion, the market itself is an emotional entity. It floats on the emotions of fellow investors. How much is a stock worth? Whatever investors are willing to pay for it. So, intrinsic value has little to do with it when investors feel they won't make a profit.

That anomaly is what allowed bubbles, such as the tech bubble of the 1990s and the more recent housing bubble that burst in 2007 to exist. Inflated values.

So, to put it in a word, the yearly DALBAR studies all point to individual investor psychology as the main reason why they leave so much money on the table. How much money? That's an interesting question.

The S&P did pretty well in 2014, returning 13.69 percent. But, according to DALBAR, the average equity mutual fund investor only garnered 5.50 percent, leaving 8.19 percent of the available gain on the table. Stretching back 20 years, the S&P returns averaged 9.85 percent. Individual investors only reaped 5.19 percent.[10]

Another factor that hampers the efforts of individual investors – lack of capital. The term the media likes to use for this is "missing the rally." If you are using your life's savings to invest in the stock market, of course you will "miss the rally" when you start to see what you have worked your entire life to accumulate slip away! For individuals to compete with the professionals, they must have discretionary funds with which to invest. In other words, money they can afford to lose. Money they don't need to meet expenses. Most Americans simply don't have that luxury.

So What's the Fix?

OK, Alfie. That's the problem, so what's the fix? That's where the Financial MRI comes in.

If you were having headaches and thought you were dying of a brain tumor, would you panic? Probably. Who wouldn't? And then you go and have an MRI and find out that all you have are clogged sinuses. Would the panic subside? Sure. And the only thing that changed was how you felt about the situation. Your emotions.

---

[10] Lance Roberts. Streettalk Live, report on Dalbar Quantitative Analysis of Investor Behavior. April 8, 2015. "Dalbar: Why Investors Suck and Tips for Advisors." https://www.advisorperspectives.com/commentaries/2015/04/08/dalbar-why-investors-suck-and-tips-for-advisors. Accessed Dec. 22, 2016.

Same goes for investing. When we do our Financial MRI, we let you see into your portfolio and know where you stand. If it's broken, and you are at risk, the good thing about looking at a portfolio is you can fix it! If it isn't broken, then don't fix it!

A few years ago, I was introduced to Modern Portfolio Theory through a colleague of mine, and that meeting changed everything I thought about investing.

I am big on proper asset allocation. As stated earlier, 91.5 percent of a portfolio's performance (good or bad) is based on how it is allocated. Not stock picking. Stock picking is when your golf buddy tells you to buy XYZ. Or market timing. That's when your neighbor boasts that he got in ABC at just the right time and got out at just the right time. Those things can affect the performance of a portfolio, sure, but only by a little. Asset allocation is the key. My great friend Lee Hyder uses the following illustration involving spaghetti sauce to make this crystal clear:

"Think of it this way: If you had the best spaghetti sauce known to man, and I asked you for your recipe, and you gave me your ingredients, but you did not give me the portions with which the ingredients were mixed, would it taste the same? NO! The same thing goes on with your portfolio. If you don't have the proper mixture inside your portfolio, it doesn't function at maximum efficiency."

Asset Classes

I analyze hundreds of portfolios every year. Most people think they are diversified because they may own 20 to 30 companies' stocks. What I frequently find after doing a Financial MRI on their portfolio is that many people have companies in the same classification. Most of them tilt toward large companies, such as those that make up the S&P 500.

When you think about it, the Dow Jones is composed of only 30 companies, headlined by the likes of giants such as Apple,

American Express, Boeing and Caterpillar. Thirty may sound like a lot, but it's not when you compare it to the 500 companies in the S&P. But typically, if you're in that asset class, and the S&P goes down, your portfolio is going down as well. If the S&P goes up, so will your portfolio. What's the point? The best way to position yourself is to have different asset classes inside your portfolio.

Which ones are the best to have? We don't know what the best asset class is going to be year in and year out. One year it can be small cap stocks. The next it can be large caps. So, to build an effective portfolio, you need to have many asset classes, not just two. We like the approach of picking them all and rebalancing them. If we knew which asset class was going to be the best, we would only pick that one.

The only way to tweak the knobs just right and keep them tweaked is by regular analysis. That's what we do. That's why people like myself are here.

These days, with so much volatility in the market, do-it-yourself investing makes about as much sense as do-it-yourself dentistry. You can, of course, do it yourself, but you run the risk of running off the rails. Also, you might ask yourself, if something were to happen to you, could your spouse continue doing what you are doing?

With a Vision, You Will Flourish

My good friend and co-host of the "Saving the Investor" radio and TV series, John J. Antonucci is not only a clear-thinking individual, he is also a pastor. A scripture he is fond of quoting is Proverbs 29:18: "Where there is no vision, the people perish." Only he puts it in the positive context, "Where there is a vision, people will flourish."

That's essentially what our broadcast is all about – providing a financial vision so investors won't have to work all their lives and end up with nothing. Education and information can be the bridge to entering retirement with a nest egg that will sufficiently sustain you and your family. Education and information can be the difference between pacing the floor worrying about the future and sleeping well at night, confident that the next morning will be another day you can enjoy in the sunshine of your golden years.

Once you realize that trying to time the market is an exercise in futility, and that investing is a long-term endeavor, you are able to make prudent choices. Proper asset allocation and rebalancing asset classes are two essential aspects of that strategy.

We recently had a client who, before we met him, felt compelled to spend his days, and often a good portion of his evenings, hunched over a computer screen, watching the stock market ticker, anxiously watching his holdings' share prices ebb and flow. When the market tanked in 2008, he followed the same pattern most independent investors follow in a correction – holding on for the rebound. He held on until 2011, and recovered most of what he lost. He was convinced that the bottom would drop out again in 2012, and he just couldn't stand the thoughts of losing what he had worked so hard to accumulate. So he liquidated his holdings and decided to sit on the sidelines. He was mistaken; 2012 produced strong returns in the market. But he remained on the sidelines and earned nothing.

He was not alone. Many investors behaved in a similar manner after the 2008 market crash. And when you ask why they felt that the market was in for another tumble, their reasons were usually based on something they had heard from a neighbor, a co-worker, a friend, relative or an "expert" on one of the dozens of financial cable channels out there. So our friend, who is now a client, was making emotional decisions. And it wasn't working for him.

We live today in the age of instant information. When I first began my career as a financial professional in the 1980s, we didn't have the internet. Folks got their news from magazines. By the time they read an article advising them to buy, sell or hold, it was old news. Now, at the touch of a button, we have advice coming at us from every corner. Is it any wonder investors, especially those who are tip-toeing into retirement, are confused?

We coach people to save and invest, not with knee-jerk reactions to errant and unsubstantiated advice, but with a plan in mind – a plan rooted in sound, effective methodology and strategy. The portfolios we build are rebalanced by using the new money that comes into the fund daily to buy what went down that day. Their holdings reflect more than 13,000 different companies. With that much diversity, the fund can buy whatever goes down daily without undue risk, and keep up that pattern, using the principle of dollar-cost averaging. That is the opposite of emotion-based investing, which is why it works. When those stocks rise, the investor is rewarded.

That is why we tell our investors, "Go enjoy your golf game, your kids, enjoy your day, enjoy your retirement. Your investments are being handled by a "disciplined approach" and "aggressive rebalancing."

Flipping Coins

When I am explaining why stock picking and trying to "time the market" doesn't work, I like to use the example of flipping a coin. Take a coin out of your pocket and start flipping it. What are the odds of it coming up heads? Fifty-fifty, of course. But if you flip the coin 10 times, you probably won't get exactly five heads and five tails. It wouldn't surprise me if you flipped the coin and even came up with heads seven or eight times out of 10. But does that make you an expert coin flipper? Of course not! You were just lucky, that's all.

What's the point? Sometimes what looks like a trend is merely randomness. When things happen randomly, results often repeat themselves, especially when there are only two outcomes possible. Our brains have trouble processing randomness, however. We want to believe that there is some kind of pattern when no pattern exists.

In 2010, CBS news reported that a Moscow circus chimpanzee named Lusha was given a million rubles to invest in the Russian stock market. The monkey outperformed 94 percent of Russia's mutual fund managers![11] What does that prove? Simply that (and this is something Wall Street's "experts" probably don't want you to know) Lusha, the Russian stock-picking monkey, relies on the same technique that most investment managers use. It's called LUCK!

Let's face it. Stock performance is based on news events. And news is unpredictable. So, unless you know the news before anyone else, a portfolio manager without a system like the one described above is simply speculating. What makes it worse, most portfolio managers work for high fees.

The fund managers we use in our investment planning believe in free market enterprise – supply and demand. They don't want any companies that are unregulated. So they will eliminate IPOs (initial public offerings) REITs (real estate investment trusts), etc. They use only asset classes that are "true and pure." Math and science at work instead of luck.

Is the rebalancing really necessary? Absolutely! If you are a boater, you know you can put your vessel on autopilot and it will hold its heading. But there is also wind and current to consider, both of which will cause the craft to go off the straight-line course. But if you use waypoints, keeping to a steady course is much more

---

[11] Larry Swedroe. CBS MoneyWatch. Jan. 25, 2010. "How Do You Beat 94 Percent of Mutual Funds." http://www.cbsnews.com/news/how-do-you-beat-94-percent-of-mutual-funds-join-the-circus/. Accessed Dec. 22, 2016.

efficient. It allows the autopilot to maintain both heading and course.

Questions?

As you can tell, I am both passionate and excited about investing. I find it intriguing and challenging. It is not necessarily the simplest of subject matter to discuss. I have conveyed things here as simply as I can, but if you have questions, I understand. And I would love to answer them personally for you. All you have to do is give our office a call and we will make sure you understand every little nuance of this part of keeping your retirement down the middle of the fairway and out of the rough.

Validation

*I play golf with a group on Saturdays. They like to add some fun to the game with dots for closest to the pin on par threes. The winner of the contest wins the "greenie." Let's say each dot represents a dollar. The key is to land on the green and be closest to the pin. But you do not automatically win just by being on the green in closest to the pin. You must **validate** it by putting well – a one-putt for a birdie or a two-putt for a par. If you don't do that, then you don't win the "greenie."*

I told this story on the radio not long ago to illustrate what it means to validate. Validate means to get a second opinion as a verification. Your drive to the green would indicate that you are a good golfer. But you must put it in the hole within two strokes to further prove the point.

When was the last time you validated your financial plan? Is it as good as you thought it was? A second opinion may be necessary to see if your income will last throughout your retirement. There is nothing wrong with having your current advisor's plan validated to make sure you are not paying excessive fees. In the medical field, a second opinion is an accepted practice to make sure a diagnosis is correct. The same goes with your retirement. Has your total retirement plan been validated lately?

CHAPTER FIVE

Products vs. Planning

The CERTIFIED FINANCIAL PLANNER™ Board of Standards airs what I think is a hilarious commercial, but one that makes a serious point. It's one of those hidden camera type of spots. The first thing you see is a glass wall with the very impressive sign announcing that this is the office of Miller & Koehler (completely fictitious).

"Let me talk to you about retirement," says a guy dressed in a perfectly tailored blue suit. He is talking to a couple we assume are husband and wife.

"The 401(k) is the soundest way to go," says blue suit. "Now let's talk asset allocation." You can tell he is just throwing terms out there that make him sound like he knows what he is talking about, but as we soon see, he doesn't have a clue.

Then, we are let on to the idea that this is a set up when he asks the couple, "Would you trust me as your financial advisor?"

The man and the woman he is speaking to look at each other and both agree that, yes, they would trust him as their financial advisor.

"You seem knowledgeable and professional," says the woman.

"Let's be clear here. I'm actually a DJ," says the man in the suit, clicking on a video which shows him in ultra-casual attire, long, braided hair, working at a turn table and dancing.

The unwitting participants are flabbergasted. They can't believe it. To drive the point home, blue suit gets up and dances to the beat while the video clip continues until the commercial ends.

The point is that anyone can hang out a shingle and claim to be a financial professional of some kind. That's why I suggest looking for those three letters adjacent to your financial advisor's name, indicating you are working with a CFP® professional.

What's behind those three little letters (four, if you count the registration symbol)? A lot:

Education – The CFP Board now requires extensive education in the following subjects before they will even consider certification.

- Professional conduct and regulation
- General financial planning principles
- Education planning
- Risk management and insurance planning
- Investment planning
- Tax planning
- Retirement savings and income planning
- Estate planning

Examination – Completing the coursework just makes you *eligible to register* for the CFP® Certification Exam. A two-day test is offered every quarter at various locations around the country. The test is four hours the first day, three hours the second day, followed by lunch, and then another three hours to round out the day. Those of us who have passed it can tell you the test is no walk in the park.

Experience – The CFP Board requires you to have at least three years of professional experience in the financial planning process before you can be certified. In other words, you must have at least completed an apprentice period. No greenhorns allowed.

Ethics – CFP® professionals agree to adhere to the high standards of ethics and practice outlined in the CFP Board's Standards of Professional Conduct. They must also acknowledge the board's right to enforce those rules through its "Disciplinary Rules and Procedures." Last, but not least, you must submit to and pass a thorough background check to find if you have had any industry regulatory actions against you. [12]

Anyone can go online these days and order business cards and call themselves just about anything they choose. But it reminds me of what Abraham Lincoln said one day when someone asked him how many legs a dog would have if you called the dog's tail a leg. Standing to his full 6'4" height, Lincoln scratched his bearded chin and replied studiously, "Only four. Calling the tail a leg doesn't make it one."

What is a Fiduciary?

Fiduciary – Now there's a word we don't use every day, but it is one you should know the meaning of if you are seeking or following financial advice. It comes from a Latin word meaning "truth." Some cousin words are "fidelity" and "confide." But in the financial advisory profession, it is the term for an individual who is legally obligated to put your financial interests ahead of their own, irrespective of commissions, fees or other remuneration.

A fiduciary is legally bound to offer solutions that are in the clients' best interests. As independent financial advisors, it's important to know that we are able to offer our clients many different options because we are not obligated to push a particular fund or insurance product.

---

[12] CFP Board. www.cfp.net. Accessed Dec. 22, 2016.

One Size Does NOT Fit All

There is no such thing as "one size fits all" in proper financial planning. The reason is obvious. Every individual is different. Different hopes, different dreams, different desires. Even if you had two individuals with whom everything else was identical, it would be this way, or at least it should, with their financial plan. Imagine if two individuals lived on the same street, were the same age, had the same size family, worked for the same employer, earned identical salaries and had the same net worth as each other. Unless they had identical financial goals, they would require different financial plans, because they would have separate and distinct visions of what they want their wealth to do for them. Even identical twins, who share the same DNA, have separate and distinct fingerprints.

That well illustrates why one-size-fits-all financial plans don't fly. They must be tailor-made.

The Swing or the Clubs

Pick your favorite professional golfer. Now imagine you have the opportunity to play with (a) your favorite golfer's clubs, or (b) your favorite golfer's swing. Which do you choose? The swing, of course. Why? An accomplished professional golfer could probably play great, even with lousy clubs. The secret is in the swing, or the skill.

Financial products are merely tools to get the job done. In our home, on a shelf in the garage, there sits a red toolbox I bought a few years ago. In that toolbox are some wrenches, a screwdriver or two, a hammer, pliers, fasteners and some other odds and ends. I must confess, my skill level with these instruments is limited. Unless the problem is extremely simple and straightforward, I'm calling a professional. They know what they are doing. We both may have the same tools, but a professional plumber, for example, understands pipes. A professional electrician knows the wiring system of the house and will fix what is wrong without blowing up the block. I have learned the hard way not to try to do it myself. When I do, it ends up costing me more because I have messed it up even more than it was before I attempted to fix it.

When I sit down with people to help them iron out a financial plan, financial products, such as annuities, life insurance or structured funds are the farthest thing from my mind. Don't get me wrong, we may eventually use some of those products, but not until I know the tool fits the specific needs of the client. To me, it is a violation of all that is ethical, sensible and professional to sell a product to someone without first ascertaining whether the product is what they need.

Knowledge Is Key

To illustrate the point, I remembered the time I played a round at Pebble Beach. It was amazing. It was everything I thought it would be, but better. It was a very windy day. Because Pebble Beach is a difficult course, our group found it wise to hire a caddie. Not to carry our clubs, but for the wisdom and knowledge he possessed about the course. These guys are more like golf coaches than caddies.

On the seventh hole, a par three overlooking the ocean, I stood on the tee box, the wind off the Pacific whipping my pants like flags. It was 100 yards from the tee to the pin. For me, that is usually a 56 wedge. But before I reached for the club, I consulted the professional caddie.

"Nope. Not on this hole," he said, and handed me my lob wedge, which is a 60-yard club. "And hit it with a ¾ swing."

"Really?" I said. "Even in this wind?"

He gave me a "trust me" nod of the head and I hit the ball. What a beautiful sight to see that white Titleist sail in the direction of the deep blue Pa-

cific, waves breaking in the distance, and then drop down almost 100 feet and plop onto the green. I two-putted for a par. It would be one of the few holes I parred that day.

There is an old expression in golf, "Let the club do the work." In other words, don't try to muscle the ball by swinging too hard. It will destroy your accuracy. Recognize the fact that it is the club that gets the ball there, not your arm strength. What I learned from this experience is that, just because the distance might say 100 yards that doesn't mean you use a 100-yard club. Because of the elevation and wind, this hole required a lob wedge. The caddie knew this because he had visited this hole hundreds of times. He had observed my swing. He could predict the effect the wind would have on the ball and knew within a few feet of where the ball would likely land. It was that caddie's knowledge that made me successful on that hole.

Every day is going to be different, even if you are playing the same course, which is one of the reasons why I love the game. Economic conditions will change from day to day. The stock market will always be up and down and full of surprises. Nothing we can do about that. It's the knowledge of how to navigate through those changes that counts.

CHAPTER SIX

The Disappearing Pension

What does an extinct automobile have to do with pensions? Quite a bit, actually. The Studebaker was a hot car back in the 1950s. It was sleek and fast. In many respects, it was ahead of its time, as it was the first production automobile to have such things as seatbelts and padded dashboards. They were reliable cars with style and power. But for some reason, the American public just fell out of love with them in the 1960s and the automaker fell on hard times. Studebaker was forced to close down one plant after another and lay off thousands of workers. The last Studebaker rolled off the line on March 16, 1966.

In the middle of all of this, their executives discovered they had another major financial problem – their pension plans were poorly funded. They would not be able to keep their promises. Many of the laid-off workers, expecting their pensions to kick in, got zilch. Others received pennies on the dollar. Auto workers had a strong union and they weren't about to take that lying down, so their union representatives complained loudly to Congress.

A general recession in the early 1970s caused other large corporations to default on their pensions. Congress responded with the Employee Retirement Income Security Act of 1974 (ERISA), which aimed to regulate pension plans. Now, it would be against the law to renege on pension promises. With the tougher regulations, companies just started phasing them out altogether.

A seismic shift was taking place when it came to the way Americans viewed retirement. It used to be you worked for the same company for 30 to 40 years, and when you retired, you could count on a gold watch and a guaranteed paycheck – usually a portion of your previous salary – coming in for the rest of your life. All that changed with pensions becoming an endangered species. With the birth of ERISA, there came something new called the do-it-yourself individual retirement account (IRA), and another program that sounded like a vitamin supplement – the 401(k), which could be sponsored and administrated by your employer. These were created by Congress to incentivize workers to put aside money themselves for their retirement. The incentive was tax-deferment. Every dollar you contributed to your plan (up to a limit set by the IRS) was a dollar that Uncle Sam didn't tax you on until you withdrew it. Pensions were called "defined-*benefit* programs." These new employer-sponsored plans were called "defined-*contribution* plans."

The main difference, of course, was that simple word, "guaranteed." The pension plans were supposed to be iron-clad, and were guaranteed by the companies that offered them for the life of the employee. You did nothing to manage them. These new plans were invested in the stock market, primarily in mutual funds. They were dependent on the returns of investments you selected. There are no guarantees with 401(k)-type plans.

So there was good news and bad news. The good news was these plans allowed investments to grow tax-deferred. With no taxes coming out, the account could accrue interest quicker and compounding was accelerated. The bad news was that you were now responsible for managing your own investments. During market crashes, such as the one that occurred in 2008, retirement accounts are hit with losses just like the rest of the stock market. For someone on the cusp of retirement, that can be a big "ouch!"

Tax-deferred is not tax-free, either. Uncle Sam is no fool. The government will get its slice of the pie (and it hopes a much bigger one) when the time comes for you to withdraw the money. And just to make sure you *do* withdraw the money, the government put something in place called required minimum distributions (RMDs), which forced you to withdraw an ever-increasing percentage of these tax-qualified accounts as soon as you reached age 70 ½.

IRAs have become very popular. Millions of Americans have pumped trillions of dollars into them. IRA owners were delighted to see their taxes shrink and their retirement savings compound quicker during the accumulation phase of their lives. But when they enter the distribution phase of retirement, or what I prefer to call the harvesting phase, they discover the IRA has a little more complexity than they first imagined. Passing their assets on to their heirs can be tricky. If you don't do it intelligently, the IRS can claim almost half of it for the tax coffers.

The part of the Internal Revenue Service code that deals with IRAs is Publication 590, or "Pub 590" for short. The document is 110 pages long, and contains the latest rules for IRAs. Ed Slott, a leading IRA expert, says in *"The Retirement Savings Time Bomb... and How to Defuse It,"* his book, "Due to a complex combination of distribution and estate taxes that kick in at retirement or death, millions of you are at risk of losing much – perhaps even most – of your retirement savings."

Variations Emerge

Over time, Congress has enacted legislation that has created variations in tax-deferred retirement accounts such as IRAs, 401(k)s, 403(b)s and the like. The most significant has been the emergence of the **Roth** IRA and **Roth** 401(k), named for the late

U.S. Sen. William V. Roth, a fiscal conservative who sponsored the legislation. Sen. Roth also co-authored the Economic Recovery Tax Act of 1981. He maintained that the less we have to pay in taxes, the more we will spend and save, which would, in turn, stimulate the economy. This, he claimed, would generate more revenue for the government in the long run than a direct tax would. The Taxpayer Relief Act of 1997, which was his idea, allows you to pay the taxes on the front end of a Roth IRA and 401(k), which in turn allows your investments to grow and be distributed tax-free. Today, Roth IRAs can be set up at many financial institutions and insurance companies, and more and more employers are offering Roth 401(k)s. They allow for early withdrawal of your original contribution (not the earnings) without penalties after a five-year waiting period. The earnings generated from the original Roth IRA contribution can also be withdrawn early, but they are subject to penalties.

I have given you a broad-brush explanation here. Rules are constantly changing, so see me in person or anyone at Advantage Retirement Group for a more detailed explanation or to answer any questions you may have.

Stay Focused on Your Goal

Keep in mind, retirement is the back nine holes of an 18-hole round. It's a time to remain alert and keep your focus. During the accumulation phase of your financial life, you work hard to put money into the aforementioned accounts. You watch it grow, and hopefully reach your savings goal. When the preservation and distribution phase kicks in, you want to keep as much as you can of what you have earned, and use the amount you need to maintain your current lifestyle. Since the rules are constantly changing, it will pay to be diligent in keeping up with them, or having a financial coach who knows what types of accounts exist and who can advise you about how to utilize them.

Replacing the Disappearing Pension

Back when I first got into the financial services profession in 1983, cellular phones and the internet didn't even exist! If someone said "cable TV" you thought they meant that wire that went from the television to the outside antenna!

Nowadays, we are living in the information age. Or, as I call it, the information *overload* age. I mean, we are inundated with opinions from every angle. Talking heads on the financial channels seem to make a sport out of disagreeing with one another on what you should and shouldn't do with your money.

In those days, you worked for a certain number of years, and you saved a certain amount of money and you *knew* how much you would have for retirement. Not so today. These days, you have to invest prudently and keep on top of it, because you are responsible. You've got to do it right. During the accumulation phase, when you are working, you are putting your wealth in the hopper, so to speak. You are going to invest differently in that phase because you are still working. But when you retire – and this is what a lot of people don't seem to understand fully – you will be taking the fruits of your labor and endeavoring to make sure they last as long as you do.

That's one of the reasons we call our radio and television shows "Saving the Investor." Saving the investor from what? From the possibility they will fall prey to the dangers of bad advice, bad timing and bad decisions that could threaten their financial security. You don't want to have to go back to work, yet that is what many have to do who have not planned properly.

The tsunami of information spouted out by the media, by advertisers and money magazines can serve to overwhelm instead of educate. Our goal on "Saving the Investor" is to cut through the fog with straight talk and common sense.

In the previous chapter of this book, we talked about disappearing pensions. If you have a pension, then consider yourself one of the fortunate few. Most of the people I meet with these days know what they are because their father or grandfather had one. Or they know someone who retired with a pension. These days, the adage comes to mind: If it is to be, it's up to ME! That's right, you have to find a way to create your own pension – or guaranteed lifetime income – if the company you work for hasn't seen fit to provide you with one.

Also, in the previous chapter, we discussed at great length why IRAs and 401(k)-type plans are great, but they are not pensions. Why? Because they are not guaranteed for life. One of the best tools for creating your own "pension" is the annuity.

Annuity Bias

Some people swear by them and some people swear at them, but there is nothing scary about annuities. They are merely a financial tool like so many others that can be used to provide a financial strategy to solve a problem – in this case, the need for a lifetime income stream. So why is it that when you say the "A" word, some people want to hide under a rock, or worse, pick up the rock and try to hit you with it.

We mostly fear what we don't understand.

Just for fun, I once asked an audience I was giving a talk to about income planning what they would think of a financial product that would perform the following functions:

- Provide protection of principal from market losses
- Offer tax-deferred interest earnings to accelerate growth
- Interest earnings linked to upside market performance
- Hold its value and not go down when the market declined
- Provide an option for guaranteed lifetime income in retirement
- Able to pass unused portion to heirs upon one's death
- Potential to avoid probate process

When I asked for a show of hands as to how many would like a financial product such as the one I had just described, almost every hand went up. Then, I asked how many in the room liked annuities, and only a few hands went up. What I had described to them was a fixed index annuity with an income rider attached – a perfectly good solution to a financial problem in some cases.

When I asked why some did not raise their hands before they knew that what I had just described was an annuity, the answers I received told me that this audience was probably representative of most individuals – they simply did not understand them. Granted, they are not for everyone, but it doesn't hurt to understand how they work.

An Explanation and History

Origin – The word "annuity" comes from the Latin words "annu" or "annus," which means "yearly" or "annually." We get our English words "annual" and "anniversary" from the same root.

In the days of ancient Rome, soldiers pooled their money before going into battle so their widows and children would be cared for if they died. Paying the money out in a lump sum was life insurance, although they didn't call it that. Paying the money out in payments for the lifetime of the family was an annuity.

An annuity is a contract purchased by an individual from an insurance company. An annuity is typically used in retirement to secure an income for the remainder of your life, or to pay a fixed number of payments over a set period of time. Not all annuities are the same. A good example would be that all annuities are contracts, but not all contracts are annuities. All Fords are automobiles, but not all automobiles are Fords. Some annuities are as different from each other in what they do as a motorcycle is from a dump truck.

There are three basic ways to categorize an annuity:

1. Is it **fixed** or **variable?** This determines **how the annuity earns interest or is invested.** Fixed annuities are considered "safe" because the principal is protected by the insurer. Variable annuities are invested directly in the stock market, and the principal is exposed to market risk, just like any other market investment.

2. Do you want income **now** or **later?** This establishes if the annuity, and thus the income, is deferred (income later) or immediate (income now).

3. Is the annuity **single premium**, or **flexible premium**? This determines whether additional funds can be added to the contract.

There are four parties to an annuity:

The contract owner. The contract owner is the person who has purchased the annuity. The contract (annuity) owner:

- Pays the premium for the annuity.
- Signs the application and agrees to abide by the terms of the contract.
- Chooses who the other parties of the contract will be.
- Can withdraw money from the contract (according to the terms).

- May add funds to the contract if it is a flexible annuity.
- Is responsible for any taxes that are due when such withdrawals are made.
- May terminate the contract.
- Is responsible for selecting contract options from an available selection.
- May change beneficiaries.

The annuitant. This can be a little confusing. The annuitant *can* be the contract owner, but does not have to be. Think of the annuitant in terms of life insurance. With life insurance, if the person who is insured dies, then the contract terminates. With an annuity, the annuitant is the *measuring life* of the contract. An annuitant is the person to whom annuity payments are made and during whose life an annuity is payable. So, until the contract owner makes a change, or until the person named as annuitant dies, the terms of the annuity remain in force. The annuitant, then, is like the insured in a life insurance policy. The annuitant can be anyone: you, a spouse, parent, child or other relative. The annuitant must be an individual with a calculable lifespan, so it cannot be a trust, corporation or partnership.

The insurer. An annuity is always a contract between an individual or individuals, or a trust, and an insurance company (the insurer). This applies whether you buy the annuity from an independent agent, a bank, or directly from the insurance company. The contract governs what can and cannot be done with the money you placed with the insurance company and the benefits you stand to receive from the contract. The wording in the contract will also spell out the rates, guarantees, limitations, costs and charges, as well as any rules governing premium payments and withdrawals.

The beneficiary. The beneficiary of an annuity is similar to beneficiaries of other investments or insurance policies. Upon the annuitant's death, the beneficiary receives the contract's specified death benefit. The beneficiary cannot change or control the contract. He or she has no say in how funds are allocated (if applicable). The beneficiary only benefits from an annuity upon the annuitant's death. A beneficiary can be a child, spouse, friend, relative, trust, corporation or partnership. An annuity can have multiple beneficiaries with varying percentages payable to each, equaling 100 percent. The contract owner can change beneficiaries at any time and the consent of a beneficiary is not necessary for changes to be made.

Types of Annuities

Annuities can be split into two main categories: *immediate* and *deferred.*

A deciding factor for choosing the annuity type you want will be based on your income needs and the flexibility desired. Do you want income now or in a few years? Do you want access to a lump sum of money? Would you like the largest possible income? These are just a few of the questions you would need to think through before purchasing an annuity.

Immediate Annuity

If you purchase an immediate annuity you are essentially trading a lump sum of money for an income stream. For example, you may give an insurance company $100,000 in return for $500 per month for the rest of your life – regardless of how long you live. The amount of income would be based on your age.

You also could have payments sent to you for a specified number of years. The amount of income would be based on interest rates and the number of years you want income. In any case, you can have the checks sent to you monthly, quarterly, semi-annually, or annually. (I am not a big fan of this type of annuity. I think you lose too much control. Once you trade your lump sum of money for an income stream, the insurance company does not allow you to access the remaining funds.)

Deferred Annuity

Deferred annuities are contracts designed to provide you with supplemental income for retirement or other long-term needs. The flexibility of deferred annuities, whether fixed or variable, is the main attraction.

With deferred annuities, there are three different types you can use depending on your needs and long-term objectives. You can purchase a fixed rate, fixed index or variable annuity.

With most deferred annuities, there is a period of time during which the funds can be subject to surrender charges. The charges are incurred only if funds are withdrawn in excess of the free withdrawal percentage stipulated by your contract. Most annuities allow the owner to withdraw up to 10 percent each year without incurring a surrender charge. The surrender charge period is stated in the contract and is typically five to 10 years. The surrender charge gradually decreases to zero over the specified period. Withdrawals will reduce the contract value and will be subject to ordinary income tax and, since, as I said, this is designed for the long term, if you withdraw your funds before age 59 ½, you might be subject to an additional 10 percent tax penalty.

Deferred Annuity Types

As I mentioned earlier, there are three types of deferred annuities: fixed rate, fixed index and variable. Let's look at the basics of each.

Fixed-Rate Annuities

Like other fixed-rate products, a fixed-rate annuity provides the contract owner with a guaranteed rate of interest. These credit interest in a manner that is most similar to the way banks credit interest on CDs. When you purchase a CD from a bank, the interest you receive usually depends on the time commitment; the longer the commitment, the higher the interest rate. A fixed-rate annuity operates in a similar way. Just like interest rates differ on CDs from band to bank, the interest rates on fixed-rate annuities will vary from insurance company to insurance company. Annuity guarantees are backed by the financial strength of the insurance company and its ability to pay claims.

The most common time horizons for fixed-rate annuities are one, three or five years. When you invest in a CD, the interest rate is locked in for a specified time. The same is true with a fixed-rate annuity. The interest the annuity earns can be withdrawn by the contract owner (subject to limitations) or left in the annuity to maximize interest compounding.

Fixed-rate annuities are popular with individuals who want to keep their principal safe from market losses. With this type of annuity, you will know exactly what to expect each year in interest. Fixed-rate annuities work great for conservative investors or those who want to know exactly what they will have earned at the end of a specific timeframe.

Fixed Index Annuities

Fixed index annuities are a hybrid product. They combine the safety of principal with interest earnings linked to a market index (such as the S&P 500, Dow Jones, NASDAQ, Russell 2000, EURO STOXX 50, etc.). Fixed index annuities have been offered in the U.S. since the mid-1990s. They have all the features of most fixed-rate annuity contracts except that the interest a contract earns is determined by the performance of the index to which the annuity is linked. While the annuity is not actually participating in the market, when the index performs well, interest is credited up to a predetermined amount, called a "cap," based on that performance.

Capped gains are a tradeoff for no losses. If the market goes up 20 percent in one year, your capped gains may be only 6 percent, but you are insulated from losses if the market loses 30 percent the following year. This protects your base. In a fixed index annuity, the worst you can do in a given year is make zero percent. This protection is why fixed index annuities have been popular with investors as of late.

One main drawback of fixed index annuities is their complication. There are more than a few moving parts in this financial instrument. There are several methods for calculating interest, for example. The fine print is not necessarily damning, there is just a lot of it. This has steered many away from using them. If you decide to use a fixed index annuity, choose one that is easy for you to understand and make sure your financial advisor explains it thoroughly to your satisfaction. If you are moving a large amount of money, and if that money represents years of your hard work, your blood, sweat, toil and tears, then make sure you understand where you are putting it and why you are putting it there. You should be as comfortable with that decision as you are that your left foot is in your left shoe. Make sure your advisor explains all the details and is able to support in writing the answers to all your questions.

Variable Annuities

For individuals who have a higher risk tolerance, variable annuities offer an alternative. When you invest in a variable annuity, you control how your funds are invested in the annuity. Under the umbrella of a tax-deferred annuity there are usually many types of separate accounts (i.e. mutual funds) in which to invest. The contract owner can allocate their money from sub-account to sub-account. (Some variable annuity contracts limit the frequency of movements.) With a variable annuity, you typically are investing in the stock market or bonds; therefore, there is risk of loss. If the investment does well, you receive all the benefit minus any fees. If the investment performs poorly, you can lose gains and even principal. In addition to surrender charges and possible income tax penalties, there are several fees associated with a variable annuity. Most have mortality and expense risk charges, sub-account expenses and administrative fees. These fees can vary from one variable annuity to another and can be very costly.

These fees can come as a big surprise if you are unaware of how they are charged. One of my clients had a variable annuity and he was absolutely sure that he was paying no fees. As it turns out, his advisor did not explain it to him. We called the company and he listened firsthand as the company representative on the other end of the line explained to him that his $500,000 variable annuity was costing him 4.7 percent in hidden fees, or almost $25,000 per year. That amounted to almost $250,000 over a 10-year period.

Which Annuity May Be Right for You?

The fact is that fixed-rate, fixed index and variable annuities are all very popular. Annuities are not appropriate for everyone and will depend on your time horizon, your other current investments, your goals and objectives, and your personal risk-tolerance level.

Unfortunately, annuities have been given a bad name. I've found many advisors who try to use them as a one-size-fits-all solution. Before even thinking about an annuity, we go through a series of questions to understand what your income needs are. Annuities are a tool that could be a great fit for part of a retirement plan when there is an income gap, either now or in the future.

As all financial vehicles do, annuities have pros and cons. Take your time and clearly know why you are choosing any investment or insurance vehicle. Work with an advisor you trust and who will be patient enough to answer all of your questions. I believe if they are used correctly and in the right circumstances, annuities can be a very useful tool for part of your retirement.

CHAPTER EIGHT

The Problem with
Average Returns

W all Street and Main Street have different ways of calculating average rates of return. This could be a major deal breaker during your retirement years. If you are an investor looking a secure retirement, this might be one of the most important chapters in the book, because it exposes the Wall Street method of calculating average returns.

Mutual funds are well known for calculating their annual returns on an *average* basis over 5-year, 10-year, 15-year and 20-year periods of time, or even since the fund's inception date. After you read this chapter, I think you will see how crucial it is to think carefully about picking funds based on these calculations.

The Tale of Two Accounts

Let's pretend you have two accounts, each with a cool $1 million at your disposal to invest. With Account A you pick a very hot company and buy $1 million worth of its stock and it returns an astounding 60 percent.

With Account B, you are more careful. This is a diversified portfolio that didn't do too badly either – it only returned 30 percent. You are on a roll! But, as the old saying goes, what goes up must come down.

The second year, your hot stock that was up 60 percent takes a beating and Account A loses 40 percent. Your diversified portfolio, Account B, fares better, losing only 10 percent.

Now, let's do the math for account A: 60 percent minus 40 percent equals 20 percent, right?

Now for account B: 30 percent minus 10 percent equals 20 percent.

Both accounts *averaged* a 10 percent annual gain (20 percent divided by two years). But look at the accounts more closely. Account A started with $1 million. The gain of 60 percent put the account up to $1,600,000 after year one. Account B started with $1 million, but had a 30 percent gain, which put the account up to $1,300,000 after year one. Then both accounts had a setback. Account A lost 40 percent, so if we take 40 percent from $1,600,000, it leaves account A with $960,000

Account B lost 10 percent. Take 10 percent from $1,300,000, which leaves us $1,170,000.

Two accounts had the same *average* rate of return, but experienced very different outcomes. Wall Street calculates average rates of return by dividing the returns by the number of years the funds have been in existence. This is what I call "fuzzy math." That doesn't help you make sure the accounts you are choosing for your retirement or investments are the appropriate ones, does it? The fact that the *average* was the same on both accounts had no bearing on the outcome of your money inside those accounts.

Averages can be tricky.

If I put one foot in ice water and the other in hot water, on *average* I'm comfortable, right? No, I'm not!

I saw a cartoon once of a man wading across a pond. The sign at the edge of the water said, "Average Depth: 3 feet." The man was struggling to keep his head above water, however, because he had stepped into a hole. Sure, the *average* depth may have been 3 feet, but the man was drowning, nonetheless.

And If I tell you that Bob and Susan ride their bikes an average of 70 miles per week, you may get the *impression* of a lovely couple riding their bikes together down a shady country lane, when the *reality* may be that Susan rides 20 miles every day while Bob sleeps late. Red flags go up when I hear the words "average" and "returns" in the same sentence.

Let's take ourselves back in time to the time span of 2000 to 2015. Why would we pick those years? I'm about to show you. But first let me ask you a question. If I were going to demonstrate the performance of a particular portfolio, would you say it would be more accurate to pick the best 15 years, or the 15 years that would represent both the good times and the bad times too? The latter, of course.

Portfolio 1 is an account that is an index fund that tracks the S&P 500. It has low fees. Portfolio 2 has much higher fees, but is a well-diversified account. Both accounts have had very similar returns over the last 15 years. The S&P 500 index fund (Portfolio 1) returned 5.68 percent over that 15-year period, and the well-diversified portfolio had a 5.68 percent return. Many people, because they want to be comfortable with what they're getting into, would lean toward the S&P 500 index. It has been around for a long time and the fees are low compared to Portfolio 2. But would that be the best decision? Let's take a look at how these two accounts fared from 2000 to 2015. As you can see in the following chart, both portfolios started with $1 million. And, as you can see they each earned nearly the same *average* return. So why does Portfolio 1, which was invested in the S&P index fund, after 15 years contain almost $500,000 less than the diversified portfolio?

VOLATILITY VS RETURNS – WHICH IS MORE IMPORTANT?

			Portfolio 1		
Year	Gains	Beg. Bal.	Earnings	Withdraw	End Bal.
2000	-9.06%	$1,000,000	-$90,600	$0	$909,400
2001	-12.02%	$909,400	-$109,310	$0	$800,090
2002	-22.15%	$800,090	-$177,220	$0	$622,870
2003	28.50%	$622,870	$177,518	$0	$800,388
2004	10.74%	$800,388	$85,962	$0	$886,350
2005	4.77%	$886,350	$42,279	$0	$928,629
2006	15.64%	$928,629	$145,238	$0	$1,073,866
2007	5.39%	$1,073,866	$57,881	$0	$1,131,748
2008	-37.02%	$1,131,748	-$418,973	$0	$712,775
2009	26.49%	$712,775	$188,814	$0	$901,589
2010	14.91%	$901,589	$134,427	$0	$1,036,016
2011	1.97%	$1,036,016	$20,410	$0	$1,056,425
2012	15.82%	$1,056,425	$167,126	$0	$1,223,552
2013	32.18%	$1,223,552	$393,739	$0	$1,617,290
2014	13.51%	$1,617,290	$218,496	$0	$1,835,786
2015	1.25%	$1,835,786	$22,947	$0	$1,858,734

Average Return: 5.68 percent

Standard Deviation: 18.61 percent

DISCLAIMER: The above table is intended to illustrate the potential results of a hypothetical investment of $1,000,000 in the Vanguard 500 Index Inv (VFINX) beginning on the first trading day of 2000 and held through the last trading day of 2015. It is assumed that any dividends and other earnings are reinvested and no allowances for external advisory fees have been made. The results may vary significantly if the beginning day and/or the ending day is altered. The holdings composing the fund have changed over time and are likely to change in the future. The fund performance and other information was acquired from Morningstar Direct. It is believed to be accurate but has not been independently verified. Past performance is not necessarily indicative of future results.

VOLATILITY VS RETURNS – WHICH IS MORE IMPORTANT?

		Portfolio 2			
Year	Gains	Beg. Bal.	Earnings	Withdraw	End Bal.
2000	8.62%	$1,000,000	$86,200	$0	$1,086,200
2001	-2.93%	$1,086,200	-$31,826	$0	$1,054,374
2002	3.43%	$1,054,374	$36,165	$0	$1,090,539
2003	15.28%	$1,090,539	$166,634	$0	$1,257,174
2004	8.54%	$1,257,174	$107,363	$0	$1,364,536
2005	8.57%	$1,364,536	$116,941	$0	$1,481,477
2006	5.49%	$1,481,477	$81,333	$0	$1,562,810
2007	10.14%	$1,562,810	$158,469	$0	$1,721,279
2008	-0.77%	$1,721,279	-$13,254	$0	$1,708,025
2009	3.41%	$1,708,025	$58,244	$0	$1,766,269
2010	11.88%	$1,766,269	$209,833	$0	$1,976,102
2011	11.18%	$1,976,102	$220,928	$0	$2,197,030
2012	5.59%	$2,197,030	$122,814	$0	$2,319,844
2013	-1.83%	$2,319,844	-$42,453	$0	$2,277,391
2014	9.61%	$2,277,391	$218,857	$0	$2,496,248
2015	-5.35%	$2,496,248	-$133,549	$0	$2,362,699

Average Return: 5.68 percent
Standard Deviation: 5.92 percent

DISCLAIMER: The above table is intended to illustrate the potential results of a hypothetical investment of $1,000,000 in a hypothetical mix of securities, which would yield a series of returns that are less volatile than the returns of an investment intended to track the S&P 500 over the same time period, beginning on the first trading day of 2000 and held through the last trading day of 2015. The table does not represent the results of an investment of an actual security or mix of securities.

THE IMPACT OF VOLATILITY WHEN TAKING INCOME

Portfolio 1					
Year	Gains	Beg. Bal.	Earnings	Withdraw	End Bal.
2000	-9.06%	$1,000,000	-$90,600	-$50,000	$859,400
2001	-12.02%	$859,400	-$103,300	-$50,000	$706,100
2002	-22.15%	$706,100	-$156,401	-$50,000	$499,699
2003	28.50%	$499,699	$142,414	-$50,000	$592,113
2004	10.74%	$592,113	$63,593	-$50,000	$605,706
2005	4.77%	$605,706	$28,892	-$50,000	$584,598
2006	15.64%	$584,598	$91,431	-$50,000	$626,029
2007	5.39%	$626,029	$33,743	-$50,000	$609,772
2008	-37.02%	$609,772	-$225,738	-$50,000	$334,035
2009	26.49%	$334,035	$88,486	-$50,000	$372,520
2010	14.91%	$372,520	$55,543	-$50,000	$378,063
2011	1.97%	$378,063	$7,448	-$50,000	$335,511
2012	15.82%	$335,511	$53,078	-$50,000	$338,589
2013	32.18%	$338,589	$108,958	-$50,000	$397,547
2014	13.51%	$397,547	$53,709	-$50,000	$401,255
2015	1.25%	$401,255	$5,016	-$50,000	$356,271

Average Return: 5.68 percent

Standard Deviation: 18.61 percent

DISCLAIMER: The above table is intended to illustrate the potential results of a hypothetical investment of $1,000,000 in the Vanguard 500 Index Inv (VFINX) beginning on the first trading day of 2000 and held through the last trading day of 2015., with $50,000 withdrawn from the investment on an annual basis. It is assumed that any dividends and other earnings are reinvested and no allowances for external advisory fees have been made. The results may vary significantly if the beginning day and/or the ending day is altered. The holdings composing the fund have changed over time and are likely to change in the future. The fund performance and other information was acquired from Morningstar Direct. It is believed to be accurate but has not been independently verified. Past performance is not necessarily indicative of future results.

THE IMPACT OF VOLATILITY WHEN TAKING INCOME

Portfolio 2					
Year	Gains	Beg. Bal.	Earnings	Withdraw	End Bal.
2000	8.62%	$1,000,000	$86,200	-$50,000	$1,036,200
2001	-2.93%	$1,036,200	-$30,361	-$50,000	$955,839
2002	3.43%	$955,839	$32,785	-$50,000	$938,625
2003	15.28%	$938,625	$143,422	-$50,000	$1,032,046
2004	8.54%	$1,032,046	$88,137	-$50,000	$1,070,183
2005	8.57%	$1,070,183	$91,715	-$50,000	$1,111,898
2006	5.49%	$1,111,898	$61,043	-$50,000	$1,122,941
2007	10.14%	$1,122,941	$113,866	-$50,000	$1,186,807
2008	-0.77%	$1,186,807	-$9,138	-$50,000	$1,127,669
2009	3.41%	$1,127,669	$38,454	-$50,000	$1,116,122
2010	11.88%	$1,116,122	$132,595	-$50,000	$1,198,718
2011	11.18%	$1,198,718	$134,017	-$50,000	$1,282,734
2012	5.59%	$1,282,734	$71,705	-$50,000	$1,304,439
2013	-1.83%	$1,304,439	-$23,871	-$50,000	$1,230,568
2014	9.61%	$1,230,568	$118,258	-$50,000	$1,298,826
2015	-5.35%	$1,298,826	-$69,487	-$50,000	$1,179,339

Average Return: 5.68 percent
Standard Deviation: 5.92 percent

DISCLAIMER: The above table is intended to illustrate the potential results of a hypothetical investment of $1,000,000, with $50,000 withdrawn from the investment on an annual basis, in a hypothetical mix of securities, which would yield a series of returns that are less volatile than the returns of an investment intended to track the S&P 500 over the same time period, beginning on the first trading day of 2000 and held through the last trading day of 2015. The table does not represent the results of an investment of an actual security or mix of securities.

The answer is because the S&P 500 portfolio had major losses in the beginning of the years measured. If we were to flip the numbers, putting the year 2015 first, and the year 2000 last, the results would have been just the opposite.

When Wall Street is *averaging* these types of numbers, it doesn't matter to them when the positive or negative returns come, whether at the beginning of the time measured, or at the end. But should it matter to you? Yes, indeed! Especially if you are contemplating retirement! You don't want your portfolio to be caught with its proverbial pants down just after a recession whittles away a sizable chunk of what you have worked and saved so long and hard to accumulate, and now have to start withdrawing from at the very worst time. Now take a look back at the "Impact of Volatility When Taking Income" spread. Look what happened to these people's retirement in the S&P 500 index while taking out $50,000 each year for income.

Ask yourself, what would I have done if I had lost half my money after only three years of retirement? How would it have affected me? Stock brokers will sometimes say, "Just stay the course, it will come back." And they are right! The stock market always does rebound – eventually. But timing is crucial to retirees. If you stayed the course and rode it out like the income example shows, at the end of 2015, your $1 million portfolio would have been down to $363,000.

Let's take a look at the diversified portfolio that had the same average return as the S&P, even though the fees were higher. It *averaged* the same as the other portfolio, but it did not suffer near the amount of losses in the bad years, and did not have near the high gains that the S&P index had.

Remember, Wall Street's *averaging* does not take your personal timeline into consideration. A market crash right at the time you retire could endanger your retirement security.

Conclusion: The *amount* of your return on your investments matters much more than the *rate* of return on your investments. You can't live on *average rates of return.* I like the way the famous American humorist Will Rogers put it during the Great Depression: "I'm not so concerned about the return **on** my money as I am about the return **of** my money."

CHAPTER NINE

Estate Planning: Do It for Love

saw another clever comic strip the other day. All three frames had a drawing of a glass filled up halfway. Frame one said, "Optimist – the glass is half full." Frame two said, "Pessimist – the glass is half empty." Frame three said "Estate Planning Attorney – The IRS took half because you didn't plan."

Nobody wants to think about death and dying, but dying is a fact of life. One of these days we will join our ancestors. Like the old Hank Williams song says, "I'll never get out of this world alive." So the responsible, and loving, thing to do is plan for that eventuality. It is sensible from a financial point of view, and it makes life so much easier on those we leave behind if we take steps while we are living to communicate how we wish our assets to be transferred to our loved ones when we pass away. There are many advantages to taking care of this aspect of financial planning sooner rather than later. One is the potential to avoid probate.

What Exactly Is Probate?

The word "probate" comes from the Latin word *"probatum"* which means "providing proof." Probate is the legal process by which our worldly goods and possessions are distributed to others after we die. In an estate of some size, it becomes legally necessary to "prove the will" in a court of law before all who may have an interest in what we leave to whom. So why is it a problem?

You could say that probate is the traffic jam at the intersection of Last Will and Testament. It can become a protracted legal mess that frustrates your loved ones and makes lawyers wealthy. But, with a little planning, it doesn't have to be that way.

The law mandates that the courts in each state will govern the manner in which what you leave behind is distributed to your heirs. If the courts are involved, that means so are attorneys. Time delays can be expected. After all, the law doesn't say that the court has to be in a hurry to get this done.

How much time the probate process will take often depends on how complicated your estate is, and whether someone decides to contest your instructions. If the estate is complex, it can take years to settle things. The last time I checked, attorneys charge by the hour, and these fees are paid from your estate.

And another thing that makes us uneasy about probate – court proceedings are open to the public. That's right. Probate proceedings are often published, allowing anyone who wishes to peer into your family's private affairs. Some people think that probate only applies if you have a will. Not so. Whether or not you have a will, your estate will be subject to probate proceedings. The purpose of the process is to (a) pay your debts, and (b) distribute your assets to heirs and beneficiaries. That's one of the reasons probate proceedings are so public. That way, anyone who thinks your estate owes them something can file a claim against it. Aside from the invasion of privacy and embarrassment that could possibly result, the publicity can serve as a magnet for predators who come out of the woodwork once they hear of a large inheritance "on the block." Vendors, contractors and attorneys representing private individuals can take issue with the provisions of the will and make claims against the estate.

If you have drawn up a will, you probably selected an individual to serve as your personal representative in these actions. If you die without a will, the court will determine that detail for you. Your personal representative will be responsible for inventorying all your property and worldly belongings so a value can be placed on your estate. Before your heirs get what you leave them, your estate will first discharge the following debts and obligations:

- Funeral expenses
- Estate administration costs, such as appraisal fees and advertising costs
- Taxes and ordinary debt
- All valid claims against the estate

It is not uncommon to see long delays between the filing of the will and the distribution of funds and property to heirs. One woman told me that her husband had passed away five years ago, and his estate was still in probate. When I asked her why, she said it was because his relatives were still squabbling over the assets. When there are disputes between family members (and it happens more often than you might think), the assets of the estate are frozen while accountants and appraisers calculate, to the penny, the value of the estate's inventory. All that takes time and money.

Avoiding the Probate Trap

All that sounds pretty dire, Alfie. Is there any way around it?

I'm glad you asked! As a matter of fact, there is! That is part of what estate planning is all about. Nearly all of the evils of probate can be eliminated, or at least reduced, through proper estate planning.

First, there are the psychological benefits. If you are like most people, you shudder at the thoughts of those you leave behind having to grieve in full view of the public, or having to worry about what the courts are doing with your estate. If you plan ahead, they won't be forced to watch as the probate process erodes the value of your estate. So, what are some of the strategies that can allow you to bypass the probate process?

Trusts – One way to avoid probate is to get rid of your property. That's essentially what trusts do – they rename your property so that it is no longer legally yours, but belongs to an entity. The law allows you to control the entity, and this allows you to maintain control of your assets.

Another cartoon strip I saw on the subject of estate planning was a takeoff on the three little pigs and the big bad wolf. You know the story, of course. The big bad wolf blows down the houses of two of the pigs, because of their insubstantial construction. But the third pig's house, which was built of bricks, withstood the huffing and puffing of the lupine villain. In the cartoon, the three little pigs are shown huddled in a house made of stone blocks, each of which were labeled, "irrevocable trusts." The cartoon big bad wolf, of course, represented the taxman.

A living trust is one that goes into effect while you are still alive. If it is revocable, it means you can change your mind. Irrevocable means you can't change your mind. For the purposes of protecting your property from the tax man and probate, irrevocable trusts are stronger and hold up better under legal pressure.

Sometimes revocable trusts become irrevocable when a person dies or becomes incompetent. The biggest difference between revocable and irrevocable trusts manifest when estate taxes are involved. When you place property in an irrevocable trust, the property no longer belongs to you and is not considered part of your estate. You can see what a difference that would make in a large estate when it comes to determining how much your estate is subject to in death taxes. If you change your mind, you are returning the property to yourself, and it is considered part of your estate.

So why would anyone consider a revocable trust? What if the value of the estate is below the federal estate tax exemption, which in 2016 was $5.43 million? In that case you may not need to be concerned. Those laws are subject to change, however. A revocable living trust is a written agreement that covers three phases of your life – (a) while you are alive and healthy, (b) if you should become incapacitated, and (c) after your death.

Also, you may be setting up a trust for the purposes of helping a charity. In that case, you may want an escape hatch that allows you to change your mind if your circumstances, or that of the charity, change.

The fact is, a properly prepared trust prevails legally over a last will and testament. A word of caution: Trusts must be prepared so as to comply with the laws of the state in which the estate dwells. Otherwise your estate may not be properly protected. Any competent estate attorney will know how to properly prepare the trust to comply with state laws.

One more point – just having a trust is not enough by itself to avoid probate – you must *fund* the trust. That means you must actually change the names on the titles and deeds from individual names to the name of the trust. You must also make sure your beneficiaries to the trust are in place. That is what ensures the assets flow to those to whom you designate. To be probate-proof, the trust must own your assets. You can sign all the documents, but if you haven't funded the trust, it's an empty shell.

According to The Florida Bar, a statewide organization for Florida lawyers, a revocable trust "avoids probate by effecting the transfer of assets during your lifetime to the trustee. This avoids the need to use the probate process to make the transfer after your death. The trustee has immediate authority to manage the trust assets at your death; appointment by the court is not necessary."

Here's how their website, www.floridabar.org, describes a revocable trust:

"A revocable trust is a document (the "trust agreement") created by you to manage your assets during your lifetime and distribute the re-

maining assets after your death. The person who creates a trust is called the 'grantor' or 'settlor.' The person responsible for the management of the trust assets is the 'trustee.' You can serve as trustee, or you may appoint another person, bank or trust company to serve as your trustee. The trust is 'revocable' since you may modify or terminate the trust during your lifetime, as long as you are not incapacitated.

"During your lifetime, the trustee invests and manages the trust property. Most trust agreements allow the grantor to withdraw money or assets from the trust at any time and in any amount. If you become incapacitated, the trustee is authorized to continue to manage your trust assets, pay your bills, and make investment decisions. This may avoid the need for a court-appointed guardian of your property. This is one of the advantages of a revocable trust.

"Upon your death, the trustee (or your successor, if you were the initial trustee) is responsible for paying all claims and taxes, and then distributing the assets to your beneficiaries as described in the trust agreement. The trustee's responsibilities at your death are discussed below.

"Your assets, such as bank accounts, real estate and investments, must be formally transferred to the trust before your death to get the maximum benefit from the trust. This process is called 'funding' the trust and requires changing the ownership of the assets to the trust. Assets that are not properly transferred to the trust may be subject to probate. However, certain assets should not be transferred to a trust because income tax problems may result. You should consult with your attorney, tax advisor and investment advisor to determine if your assets are appropriate for trust ownership."

Beneficiaries – With some trusts, you can be the trust's beneficiary. That beneficiary line is one of the most important lines on many financial documents. When you say the word "beneficiary," most people think of life insurance. But many other documents, such as retirement savings accounts and IRAs, have designated beneficiaries.

I know of a case where a couple was married for 10 years and then divorced. The woman had a good job at a software company and hundreds of thousands of dollars in her 401(k). Because she neglected to change the beneficiary line on her 401(k), when she died in an automobile accident, the money went to her ex-husband and not to her children.

In another case, a man failed to update his documents and left his former wife as the sole beneficiary on a $2 million life insurance policy when he remarried. Upon his death, his widow was left with nothing while his former wife received the $2 million. Nothing could be done, because those beneficiary lines typically trump the provisions of a will.

In most cases, assets with designated beneficiaries do not have to go through the probate process. When I do document reviews for clients, one of the first things I look at is the beneficiary line. Would you believe that on some documents, hundreds of thousands of dollars are inadvertently set to be paid out to an ex-spouse? Just think of how that scenario would play out if the person who owned the assets remarries. By neglecting to update their documents, they would be disinheriting their current spouse.

I have seen some cases where the designated beneficiary line has been left blank. Sometimes it will say simply, "estate." I have also seen the word, "spouse," or "husband" or "children" on the beneficiary line. Make sure you designate your beneficiaries by name. You may wish to leave the asset to first your spouse, then equal shares to your children should your spouse die. If you don't have enough room to express all of that on the beneficiary line, use another sheet of paper and express your wishes fully. Make it clear so there will be no mistake as to what you intend. Remember, the idea of estate planning is to ensure that, when you die, your belongings and assets transfer to your heirs in the manner in which you intended while you were alive. For that to be the case, you must *legally express* your intentions.

Some account custodians may require a change of beneficiary form to update documents. These can usually be downloaded and printed out in a matter of minutes. If the beneficiary is a minor, you will need to designate an adult as administrator of the funds. That administrator is usually the person your will names as guardian, but it does not have to be. You can also create a trust and name a trustee. Insurance companies don't write checks to minors.

Joint Ownership with Rights of Survivorship – One way to make clear who gets what in an estate is to use joint ownership with rights of survivorship. Investment accounts, for example, with TOD (transfer on death) designations, allow for naming beneficiaries and are not required to go through probate. If an asset has joint ownership with right of survivorship, it passes through to the second owner when the first owner passes away. If that asset contains a TOD provision, the assets pass along to the beneficiary if both joint owners die. Either way, the asset will probably not have to go through probate.

If an individual's name is on the document as co-owner, that person continues to own the asset when the other co-owner dies. Think of a joint checking account where both the husband and wife equally own and equally control the money in the account. There is no wrangling in a probate court as to who owns that asset. Likewise, it is the same with property or an investment account when it is articulated on the documents that the asset is owned by *joint tenants with rights of survivorship*, not as tenants in common. Please see your estate attorney on this one. Laws vary from state to state.

Do You Need a Trust?

Whether you need a trust depends on a number or circumstances. You may need to establish a trust if:

- You have a complicated family situation that requires adjusted timelines. An example would be that you wish to care for your spouse first, and upon his or her death you want the rest to go to your children from a previous marriage.

- You wish to leave your assets to your heirs in such a way that it is not immediately payable to them. For example, you may wish to leave it to a son or daughter in lump sums when they achieve a life goal, such as graduation, etc.
- A sizable portion of your assets are in real estate, or a business.
- You have an heir who suffers from a disability and you wish to provide for him or her without interrupting some type of government assistance. The trust would carefully dole the money out so as not to disqualify them.

Powers of Attorney

Sam and Wanda are on vacation and they are involved in a serious automobile accident. They survive, but both are badly injured. While they will recover eventually, they learn they will have to stay in the hospital for six months or more.

Who is going to care for such things as their utility bills so the freezer stays on and the water pipes don't freeze? Who is going to collect and open their mail? If Sam and Wanda had the presence of mind to appoint someone they trust to act in their behalf, it will be no problem. It could be a son or daughter, or another trusted family member with the time and circumstances to perform the task. This is what long-term powers of attorney are for. Include such a document in your estate plan. Let the person you select for this duty know, and keep your documents in a fire-proof safe in your house.

Living Wills

When I ask clients if they have a living will, I sometimes get a blank stare. I know what they are thinking. "What is that?"

Let's face it, no one wants to talk about death and dying at a family gathering. But it is probably one of the most loving things you can do for your family. A living will expresses what you want to happen in the event you are not able to make life and death decisions for yourself. Living wills and medical directives specify health care and end-of-life decisions so your loved ones will not have to wring their hands over what you would want them to do. Along with the living will usually goes a health care power of attorney. This designates a loved one who knows you well to have responsibility to instruct doctors and nurses if you are no longer cognizant of your surroundings. Some people want artificial life support. Others may wish to have some types of life support and not others. Some may want none at all. These documents do your speaking for you when you can no longer speak for yourself.

Remember the Terri Schiavo case? She was a St. Petersburg, Florida, resident who collapsed in 1990 and was rushed to the hospital where she remained in a coma for eight years, kept alive by machines. The doctor proclaimed her brain dead, but relatives struggled with what to do. The husband finally decided to have her feeding tube removed. That would have ended her life, but her parents fought the move. The matter was left for the courts to decide and dragged out for years with the entire nation watching.

Of course, the key question was, "What would Terri have wanted?" But no one knew. She did not have a living will, which would have settled the issue quickly and spared everyone all the anguish.

Health care professionals are relieved when they see that families have these documents. They will usually ask for them before a serious operation or when someone is admitted to the hospital.

They respect the wishes of the individual, too. They are not just for the elderly and infirm. Anyone could have an accident or sudden illness at any time. It only makes sense, while you are planning, to include a living will and a durable health care power of attorney in your documents.

Estate Planning Fails

What follows are some examples of famous people who failed to plan their estates properly and the sometimes strange consequences that followed:

Leona Helmsley – Hotel heiress Leona Helmsley died in 2007 and left $12 million in a trust fund to her small Maltese lapdog, Trouble. In the process, she disinherited two grandsons who complained publicly, naturally, and the press had a field day with the news. Two other grandsons were granted $5 million each if they would promise to visit their grandfather's grave once each year. Helmsley had served 18 months in a federal prison in the 1990s for tax evasion. When her husband, hotel magnate Harry Helmsley, died in 1997, Leona bought the tiny pooch for comfort, and treated the dog to a life of luxury. Her will stipulated that when Trouble died, she would lie beside the hotel heiress in her 12,000 square-foot Helmsley family mausoleum in Westchester County, New York. Her will also stipulated that $3 million of her fortune be set aside for steam cleaning the burial crypt at least once every year. Leona hated dirt.

The dog lived another two years after Helmsley's death, and was treated like a queen. A judge reduced the dog's inheritance to $2 million, which was enough to pay $100,000 for her upkeep, which included $1,200 per year in dog food and $8,000 per year in grooming (there is no record to indicate the dog protested the ruling). Blind and in declining health, the dog was tended to by round-the-clock care at the Helmsley Sandcastle Hotel in Sarasota, Florida, until her death. Since Trouble died leaving no will, the rest of the money in her trust went to charity. Imagine what the family thought of that?[13]

Michael Jackson – When the King of Pop died in 2009 of an overdose of propofol and benzodiazepine, he left behind an estate that was far from properly planned. It was estimated that he earned around $700 million per year, but he spent so extravagantly that it was unclear even to Jackson's closest advisors what his estate was worth. His Neverland Ranch cost millions each year. It contained an amusement park and a zoo, and took as many as 150 employees to keep it running. Jackson's debts were between $400 million and $500 million at the time of his death. Jackson made implausible choices in planning his estate, choosing his aging mother to be the guardian of his children, and Diana Ross, famous former member of the Motown singing group, The Supremes, as a back-up guardian. What if their grandmother died? Would the children then move in with Diana Ross?

As this is written, the IRS is suing the estate for back taxes. The estate claims it was worth a mere $2,105 at the time of his death. The IRS contents the number to be more in the neighborhood of $434 million. The total bill could be more than $1 billion when interest, penalties and lawyers' fees are included. The estate, which benefits his mother, Katherine, and his three children, continues to make money, earning around $2 billion since his death.

Another problem with Jackson's estate was organization. He reportedly left so many investment accounts, bank accounts and documents scattered throughout the globe that getting a comprehensive snapshot of his entire estate was virtually impossible. The lesson here is to have an attorney pull your estate together for

---

[13] Susan Donaldson James. ABC News. June 10, 2011. "Leona Helmsley's Little rich Dog Trouble Dies in Luxury." http://abcnews.go.com/US/leona-helmsleys-dog-trouble-richest-world-dies-12/story?id=13810168. Accessed Dec. 22, 2016.

those you leave behind. Let trusted family members know where your important documents and assets are.[14]

James Gandolfini – When the star of the TV series "The Sopranos" died in 2013, his will directed his executors to pay any estate taxes that were due before his assets were divided up among his heirs. Liz Weston, writing in an article entitled, "Five Celebrities Who Messed Up Their Wills," which appeared Aug. 1, 2013 in MSN Money, said, "The problem is that any wealth left to his wife, Deborah Lin, could have avoided estate taxes entirely. (Although the federal estate tax can kick in on estates worth more than $5 million, you can leave an unlimited amount to a spouse without incurring a tax bill.)"

Anna Nicole Smith – The case of Vickie Lynn Marshall (stage name Anna Nicole Smith) will go down in history as one of the all-time estate nightmares. She was the former *Playboy* centerfold who married 89-year-old billionaire oil tycoon, J. Howard Marshall II, whom she met at a strip club where she worked. Marshall died 13 months after the marriage. A court battle ensued when relatives claimed that Smith was not entitled to Marshall's considerable fortune. While Smith was fighting in probate court to claim a portion of Marshall's money, she died. Her will left everything to her teen son, who had died before she did. You can imagine what a mess this was. Making matters worse, Anna Nicole Smith also had a baby before she died. The child was essentially disinherited. The lesson we can learn here is to update your wills regularly – at least once a year. When significant family events occur, such as divorces, marriages or births, re-structure your documents to accommodate them. Litigation over the estate has, at this writing, lasted more than two decades and is only just now – tentatively – considered closed.

---

[14] Parker Hall. The Sovereign Investor. April 20, 2016. "Michael Jackson's Estate Faces Billion-Dollar Legal Battle with IRS." http://thesovereigninvestor.com/asset-protection/michael-jackson-an-estate-to-die-for. Accessed Dec. 22, 2016.

Gary Coleman – You may remember the wisecracking young-ster from the TV show of the 1980s, "Diff'rent Strokes." When he died in Utah in 2010, he was not wealthy. He still had some acting royalties coming in, but he left behind conflicting wills and a puzzling note that sparked a court battle.

The first will filed in probate court was drafted in 1999, and left his estate to his former manager. The second will, signed in 2005, left everything to a friend. Adding to the confusion, he married Shannon Price in 2007 and amended the second will, making her his heir. The codicil was hand written and included these strange words: "This I have done because of my personal selfishness and weakness and I love her with all of my heart." A year later, Coleman and Price divorced. That invalidated the codicil under Utah law, but Price argued that she should have inherited the estate, which consisted of a house with a mortgage and some modest assets, because they were living together even though divorced.

Coleman slipped and fell at his home and went into a coma. Price had been given power of attorney to make medical decisions if he were incapacitated. She ordered the doctors to disconnect life support a day after the fall. A court document later surfaced that showed the 42-year-old actor had asked that he be kept alive for at least 15 days in such circumstances. Clearly, Coleman had failed to update his estate plans after a major life event (marriage and then divorce). It is a lesson to make sure those to whom you issue power of attorney will carry out your wishes.

Steve McNair – Police said that National Football League quarterback Steve McNair, 36, was murdered by his 20-year-old mistress, who then killed herself. McNair was married, but his wife apparently had no knowledge of the affair. According to police, the mistress was angered because she believed McNair had yet a third love interest.

McNair, who spent most of his time playing for the Houston Oilers and the Tennessee Titans, never drafted a will. His estate was worth almost $20 million, and was frozen during the probate process. His wife, Mechelle, mother to two of his four children, was forced to beg the court to release money to live on. McNair had built a ranch for his mother. She had lived on it for 15 years, but when she found out she would have to start paying $3,000 per month rent, she moved out.

If McNair had set up a revocable living trust, and transferred the assets to it, the estate would have been kept out of probate and the public would not have been privy to all the tawdry details surrounding his death. The takeaway for any wealthy person with minor children should be obvious. Establish trusts for them so they are cared for. And at the very least, have a will.[15]

Marilyn Monroe – Marilyn Monroe died of what was reported as a suicide (sleeping pills) in 1962. Her will was probated in New York and the proceedings were not closed until 2001. What was the problem? When the famous actress died, she was unmarried and had no children. The problem was she had left the entire estate (with the exception of $100,000 to care for her mother) to her acting coach, Lee Strasburg. The estate is now in the name of Marilyn Monroe LLC and still makes millions of dollars per year for Strasburg's widow, who barely knew Monroe. Had the blond bombshell used a revocable living trust instead of a will, her heirs could have avoided a 39-year legal battle. She could also have specified that profits from her ongoing celebrity after her death would be payable to a specific person or charity.

Phillip Seymour Hoffman – Perhaps best known for his portrayal of Truman Capote, Phillip Seymour Hoffman died of a drug overdose in 2014 and left his estate worth $35 million to his partner and mother of his three children, Marianne O'Donnell. He neglected to create trusts for the children. Because the couple was not married, he created a $15-million tax event. Had O'Donnell

---

[15] Liz Weston. MSN Money. Aug. 8, 2013. "5 Celebrities Who Messed Up Their Wills." http://www.msn.com/en-ca/news/other/five-celebrities-who-messed-up-their-wills/ss-BBaO5Hb. Accessed Dec. 22, 2016.

and Hoffman tied the knot, the estate would have been transferred tax-free. By not setting up a revocable trust, Hoffman's estate was destined to end up on probate, exposing to the public all of the family's financial information.[16]

These are just a few. The archives of Hollywood and the music world are strewn with examples of poor estate planning, procrastination and, even worse, no estate planning at all. Getting your affairs in order requires a little time and effort while you are alive but can save your loved ones much anguish and time. Planning the details of the orderly transfer of your property after your death is one of the most loving gifts you could possibly present to your family.

---

[16] Tim Lloyd. Wealth Management Today. March 5, 2015. "5 Epic Hollywood Estate Planning Fails." http://wmtoday.com/2015/03/05/5-epic-hollywood-estate-planning-fails/. Accessed Dec. 22, 2016.

A SURVIVOR'S CHECKLIST

Things that need to be done when a loved one dies
- **Keep with your important papers** -

IMMEDIATE:
- Obtain signed death certificate and autopsy records (if applicable).

- Within the first 24 hours, look for organ donation records. Check for signed authorizations and arrange immediately.

- Inventory safe deposit boxes and personal papers of the deceased. Look for burial insurance policies; prepaid mortuary or cremation society plans.

- Contact mortuary to make burial (or cremation) and funeral arrangements. Arrange for obituary notice.

- Contact friends and relatives. ALLOW YOUR FRIENDS AND FAMILY TO HELP YOU OUT IN THIS TIME OF NEED.

- Make arrangements for pets (if any).

- Cancel regular elder assistance services.

- Obtain certified copies of the death certificate from the mortuary (consider purchasing 10 to 20 copies).

WITHIN 30 DAYS:
- If applicable, notify:
  - ✓ Social Security Administration to stop checks

  - ✓ Department of Health services if the deceased was receiving Medicaid

  - ✓ Veterans Administration

  - ✓ Payers of any pensions (such as former employer), or annuities

  - ✓ Department of Motor Vehicles

- Locate documents, including: will, trust(s), insurance policies and deeds to real estate

A SURVIVOR'S CHECKLIST (CONT.)

Things that need to be done when a loved one dies
- **Keep with your important papers** -

WITHIN 30 DAYS (CONT.):
- If there was a Living Trust, contact:
  - ✓ Successor Trustee (Trust Manager) for eventual distribution of assets

  - ✓ **ADVANTAGE RETIREMENT GROUP (800-807-3847)** for review of possible death and/or income taxes owing and assistance in sorting out and distributing assets

  - ✓ Insurance companies and arrange for any death benefits to be paid to beneficiaries

  - ✓ IRA and pension companies for any death benefits to be paid to beneficiaries

- If there was NO Trust and only a will, contact:
  - ✓ County clerk and deposit the original will within 30 days

  - ✓ Executor to begin the probate process with an attorney

  - ✓ ADVANTAGE RETIREMENT GROUP (800-807-3847) for review of possible death and/or income taxes owing and assistance in sorting out and distributing assets

WITHIN 60 DAYS:
- Notify all creditors and utility companies
- Transfer title on jointly held assets
- Inventory personal effects and arrange for disposition to family members, friends or charities

WITHIN SIX MONTHS:
- IF SURVIVING SPOUSE:
  - ✓ Contact ADVANTAGE RETIREMENT GROUP (800-807-3847) for review of finances and revised financial game plan (e.g., replace a lost pension, increase safety of remaining assets, etc.)

  - ✓ Update your will or trust

CHAPTER TEN

Covering Long-Term Care

hen CBS news aired a segment recently on the top retirement fears of American seniors, you could see the worry on the faces of the people they interviewed. One woman told the reporter, "I don't believe I'm comfortable with the amount we've saved." When the reporter asked her to explain, her response focused on unexpected medical expenses. She said she knew that medical bills can wreck a family budget.

Her late mother's savings dwindled to $11,000 when she developed Alzheimer's and spent her last five years in a nursing home.

"I've seen that the cost of care in a skilled facility is rising faster than salary or savings can possibly rise," she said. "So I need to be prepared for that because none of us want to leave that bill on our kids' shoulders."

According to the report, a couple will need approximately $220,000 to cover future medical costs.[17]

---

[17] Anthony Mason. CBS Evening News. Feb. 18, 2015. "The top retirement fear of American seniors." http://www.cbsnews.com/news/high-medical-expenses-top-u-s-retirement-fears/. Accessed Dec. 22, 2016.

The Alzheimer's Association reports that about 11 percent of those over 65 have the disease, and that the estimated lifetime cost of care for someone with Alzheimer's is $174,000.[18]

If those figures are even close to accurate, then, as the commander of the endangered space capsule Odyssey said to Mission Control in the movie "Apollo 13": "Houston, we have a problem." In June 2015, the Government Accountability Office released a detailed report measuring the retirement savings of households between the ages of 55 and 64. Only 5 percent of these households have savings of more than $150,000. In fact, the vast majority of retirees in the United States are drastically under-prepared for such an eventuality as long-term care.[19]

A good estate plan will consider the possibility of long-term care. What is the probability of your needing long-term care in the later years of your life? According to the LongTermCare.gov website, "someone turning 65 today has almost a 70 percent chance of needing some type of long-term-care services and supports in their remaining years. Women need care longer (3.7 years) than men (2.2 years). One third of today's 65-year-olds may never need long-term care support, but 20 percent will need it for longer than 5 years."[20]

Which would you say is a bigger threat to our retirement nest eggs – stock market risk or long-term care? I seldom hear people telling me their parents lost everything they had saved all of their

---

[18] Elena Holodny. Business Insider. March 10, 2016. "The one threat many retirees aren't financially prepared for." http://www.businessinsider.com/financial-advisor-insights-march-10-2016-3. Accessed Dec. 22, 2016.

[19] Brian Stoffel. The Motley Fool. Feb. 22, 2016. "The Average American Household Approaching Retirement Has This Much Saved Up." http://www.fool.com/retirement/general/2016/02/22/the-average-american-household-approaching-retirem.aspx. Accessed Dec. 22, 2016.

[20] U.S. Department of Health and Human Services. "How Much Care Will You Need?" http://longtermcare.gov/the-basics/how-much-care-will-you-need. Accessed Dec. 22, 2016.

lives due to a stock market correction. But losing it all because of a nursing home confinement is all too common.

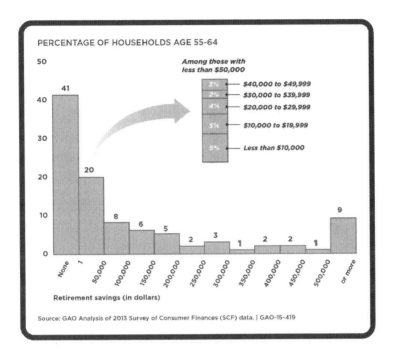

Genworth, a Fortune 500 insurance company, surveys the cost of long-term care across the United States each year. Genworth's 2016 Cost of Care Survey (conducted by CareScout®), is the most comprehensive survey of its kind and covers over 55,000 long term care providers in 440 regions nationwide. The median cost of a private room in a Florida nursing home was over $100,000 and expected to experience an annual growth rate of 4 percent! It's easy to see how that could quickly wipe out a retirement nest egg in a hurry. Other median annual Florida long-term-care rates include:

- Homemaker services - $42,328
- Home health aide - $45,188
- Adult health day care - $16,380
- Assisted living facility - $36,540
- Nursing home (semi-private room) - $89,060

To see the median cost in other states, visit https://www.genworth.com/about-us/industry-expertise/cost-of-care.html.

Long-Term Care Insurance

So why is it that, according to the American Association for Long-Term Care Insurance, only 8.1 million Americans own it? That translates to only around 10 percent of American seniors.

Cost is one factor. Let's say a couple, both age 55, want to take out a traditional long-term-care insurance policy that would pay out $162,000 for each of them, and include a 3 percent inflation option. That would cover them for almost two years in a semi-private room in an average Florida nursing home. They would have to pay $3,725 annually for the both of them to be covered.

Traditional long-term-care insurance is like auto insurance. It's a use-or-lose-it proposition. If you pay thousands of dollars into the policy over the years and never need long-term care, that money is down a black hole. Of course, you don't *want* to have to use it.

Also, there is no guarantee your rates will remain the same. An individual who is age 60, for example, might pay, say, $200 per month for a policy that provides as little as $150 per day for a maximum of three years, then be faced with a rate increase a few years down the road. If they can't afford the rate increase, they are "between a rock and hard place." If they cancel the policy, they lose all they have paid into it.

A New Approach

Insurance companies are in business to make a profit. It has not escaped their notice that that sales of traditional long-term-care insurance aren't exactly soaring. In recent years, they have come up with new and different solutions. One creative approach is to attach long-term-care options to annuities and life insurance policies. These policies are called "combos" by those in the insurance industry, because they combine two coverage elements into one.

There are many variations on this. One is a fixed annuity that provides a guaranteed minimum return (typically around 3 percent per year) with a long-term-care policy built in. If your funds are ever needed for long-term care, the amount you put in comes out first. Then a benefit is triggered that will in essence provide up to three times the amount of the annuity for long-term care. As an example, if you purchased a $100,000 annuity with a selected benefit limit of 300 percent and a two-year long-term-care benefit factor then you would have an additional $200,000 available for long-term-care expenses, even after the initial $100,000 annuity policy value was depleted. In other words, an annuity purchased with $100,000 could potentially pay out long-term-care benefits of $300,000. That is a broad-brush description of the product and provisions, which vary from one insurance company to another. But you get the idea.

Another possible solution for individuals who qualify is life insurance combined with a long-term-care (LTC) rider. These policies are usually purchased with a single premium, just like the annuity, and, on average, the premium is around one-third to half of the death benefit. The LTC benefit is usually around 2 percent of the death benefit per month.

Let's say someone bought one of these combination policies and paid a $50,000 premium into a $100,000 life policy with an LTC rider. The cash value (not the surrender value) will be in the neighborhood of $50,000. The LTC benefit would be somewhere around $2,000 per month if long-term care were needed. Whatever money is paid out reduces the policy's cash value by the same amount. In most cases, the applicant must pass a physical to qualify for the insurance.

These policies are not for everyone, and there are a few moving parts to them I have not taken the time to detail here. It is best to consult with an insurance professional for a thorough explanation. The point is that traditional LTC insurance is not necessarily the only game in town.

According to the United States Department of Health and Human Services, seven out of 10 people who live to the age of 65 will need some type of long-term-care services at some point in their lives. Let's say that you were going to fly to a tropical island for a vacation. You get to the airport and you hear an announcement informing you that seven out of 10 airplanes are not going to make it to their destinations. Would you even consider getting on board one of those airplanes? I doubt it. Yet, we take chances with our fortunes every day by not protecting ourselves in some fashion.

Some people I have discussed this with came into the office under the mistaken impression that Medicare would cover it. Medicare is a wonderful provision for seniors, but it does not pay for long-term care. Medicare Part A (hospital insurance) may cover care given in a certified skilled nursing facility if it's medically necessary, but most nursing home care is custodial care, like help bathing or dressing. Medicare doesn't cover that.

What about Medicaid? You have to be a pauper in the eyes of the government, and a ward of the state to be covered by Medicaid. If you are on Medicaid, your choices are limited as to the quality of your care. Medicaid has gotten very strict about transferring property to qualify for long-term care. They have a five-year look-back period that prevents individuals from giving all of their wealth away to their children just to get Uncle Sam to pick up the tab for the nursing home. They will insist that you "spend down" all of your money, including the value of your home equity. They let you keep $2,000 in the bank for personal items, and they monitor that closely.

So, if you don't have insurance, and you aren't covered by Medicare and Medicaid is not an acceptable option, what's left? Your personal assets and those of your family.

There may be no easy or cheap answer to this dilemma, but I advise anyone who values planning over poverty to invest the time to talk to a professional fiduciary and work out a strategy that protects you.

One thing is for certain, if you intend to insure yourself against this possibility (or probability), you need to do so before it happens. Afterward is too late. You can't dial up your insurance company and upgrade your homeowners' policy *during* a house fire. Also, your total net worth will determine to some extent the amount of protection you need. It wouldn't make sense to take out a $5 million fire insurance policy on a $1 million home. You need insurance coverage that matches what you stand to lose. The more considerable your assets are, the more you have to protect.

Procrastination is part of human nature. But the longer you wait to buy insurance to protect with long-term care insurance, the costlier it may become. Your health may decline, causing you not to qualify. The older you are, the stricter underwriting is. Also, the older you are, the more expensive it becomes, especially if you go with traditional long-term care.

If you are trying to determine if you need long-term-care insurance of any kind, ask yourself, "How would I pay for assisted living or a nursing home if I needed it right now?" At $400 per day, how long would it take for your personal assets to be depleted?

CHAPTER ELEVEN

The End Game: Finishing with the Best Score

enjoy playing the game of golf for many reasons. I know I'm not great at the game, but in many ways it's like life – there's always room for improvement. Even professional golfers will tell you they are always seeking to improve their game.

Another reason I love the game is it helps me unwind and think. I do some of my best thinking when I am focused on getting that little white ball from the tee to the green in as few strokes as possible.

A few weeks ago, a fellow golfer uttered one of those golf clichés that I must have heard a million times on the green. I had a 20-foot putt, and I suppose he meant it as encouragement.

"You drive for show and you putt for dough," he said.

The meaning of the expression is obvious. A professional golfer may impress the gallery with a long drive. But as anyone who has ever played golf knows, if you make it to the green with one long drive, and then flub the opportunity by putting three or four times before finding the cup, you are no better off.

A pro once taught me a valuable lesson: "You don't have to kill it," he said. "Hitting it a long way is not nearly as important as hitting it straight."

His other pearl of wisdom was to work on my short game twice as much as I work on my long game.

"What good does it do you if you can hit it 200 yards if you can't put it in the hole?" he said. "Chipping and putting is what makes a great golfer."

What does that have to do with finance and money management, Alfie? Just this: Decisions you make around retirement time can be likened to those strokes around the green. This is the "end game" of golf, as it were. In your early working years and your middle working years, you can afford to "blow it" a few times. You have time to recover. But decisions you make toward the end of your working years, and as you enter retirement, are critical. This is where the game becomes more intense. The consequences of foolhardy money management or errant investment decisions are greater and longer lasting. There is little to no "recovery time" for a mistake.

"It Ain't How; It's How Many"

Of all the golf one-liners that players swap on the links, the one that you usually hear after making a few ugly, but lucky, shots and parring a hole or getting a birdie is this one: "It ain't how; it's how many." In other words, it's the score you end up with that counts. That is true in retirement planning as well. It is a lifelong process. You may bumble and stumble a few times, but if you can correct course and make the right decisions closer to the end game, you can end OK.

Don't get me wrong; you should try to use sound judgment throughout your working life. I'm just saying that many people don't, for reasons having to do more with education and human nature than anything else.

Most people realize they are a "senior citizen" when they hit the double-nickel – age 55. It's when you begin qualifying for senior citizen discounts at some movie theaters and fast food places. That is also a pivotal year if you have a 401(k) and want to retire early. At age 55, you are able to make withdrawals from your 401(k) without penalty *if you are no longer working with the employer.* It's just a wrinkle in the IRS tax code that could work to your advantage. When you turn 59 ½, you can withdraw money from your retirement account without penalty even if you are still working. I don't necessarily recommend it. Every case is different.

For most Americans, full retirement age is 66. But at age 62, you can begin collecting your Social Security if you need to. That's another move I don't necessarily recommend, unless you are desperate for the money or are terminally ill. For one thing, you are reducing the monthly benefit amount you will collect for the rest of your life by as much as 30 percent. For another, your benefit will increase by around 8 percent per year the longer you wait until you hit the age of 70. After that, there is no advantage of postponing Social Security.

When you turn 65, you are eligible for Medicare – one of the best cards Uncle Sam deals you from the retirement deck. Some think they have to file for their Social Security benefits when they sign up for Medicare, but not so. You can sign up for Medicare three months before you hit your 65th birthday. Part A is hospital coverage. You don't have to pay extra for Part A if you have worked for 10 years and paid into the system. Part B is medical coverage (doctor visits, etc.) and it is not free. Most people with average incomes pay a little over $120 per month for it. For every year you are eligible and *don't* sign up for part B, you can expect to pay 10 percent more for it (there is an exception for if you qualify for a special enrollment period based on employer health coverage). Read all about it (and apply) at www.ssa.gov.

Ignorance Is Not Bliss

Golf coaches don't play the game for you. They can't improve your game for you. Only you can do that. What they do is provide you with information and education. It is up to you to change your swing, or putting stroke, or whatever other aspect of your play that will improve your score.

When it comes to financial planning, ignorance certainly is not bliss. When I sit down with people in our conference room at the Advantage Retirement Group headquarters, a lot of information is exchanged completely free of charge. It's like looking on a map and trying to find the "You Are Here" spot. We need to know where we stand and where we are before we can get to where we want to go.

As the process continues, if it continues, we will likely get into some serious number-crunching and detailed analysis of investments and income strategies. But first comes the task of totaling monthly expenses, debts and income needs. Once the current financial picture is in focus, then we can begin working on the future. Then we can set some numbers in place. The percentage we need to save from our surplus at the end of the month.

Sometimes I meet people who feel like this is similar to playing golf without knowing the score – if they don't know where they stand, they don't have to feel as anxious about each shot. If you are the winner, hey, it's a pleasant surprise. But when we're talking about three decades of life, that's not the best way to play. The people I speak with who have this attitude say the "don't tell me" approach is about feeling less anxious; yet, as they talk to me, statements of worry and concern tumble out, showing there are still unaddressed concerns under the surface.

That's precisely why it's important that you talk to a professional who is a fiduciary. They can help you understand your options, and sooner is better than later so you can correct course, if necessary, or have the confidence that you are driving in the right direction. Because it's important for you to know your score – after all, there are no retirement "mulligans."

CHAPTER TWELVE

My Brother-in-Law

would like to tell you a story about my brother-in-law, David Pavey.

David never had a bad word to say about anyone. He was the type of person who would make friends with strangers in elevators. That's just how he was. David married my sister, Toni. Their first child, David Blake, is now an advisor at Advantage Retirement Group, working out of our headquarters office in Fort Myers Florida.

A couple of years after David Blake was born, David and Toni had a second child, a daughter, Candace Santina Pavey (now Miller). Both David Blake and Candace Santina are fine young adults now and doing very well for themselves. But let's go back in time to when they were 6 and 3 years old, respectively.

Life was good. Toni was a nurse and David a nurse anesthetist. If you know anything about anesthesiology, you know the agents used by these professionals to render the patients unconscious before an operation are gasses. Whenever someone asked David what he did for a living, he would always reply, "I pass gas." It always got a laugh.

David loved to work hard. He also loved life and spending time with his family. By the time his young children were growing up, I was in the insurance and financial advisory business. I casually mentioned to David one afternoon that perhaps it would be prudent on his part to get some life insurance on himself for my sister, just in case something happened to him. He responded like most people when you bring up that subject. He said he knew it was something he needed to do, but he saw no urgency. After all, he was healthy and relatively young. It was something he would "get around to."

But because it was my sister and her two kids, I guess you could say I stayed on his case, in a nice way of course. The good news was we were able to get him a very nice-sized policy, even though he had Type 2 diabetes. The bad news came in August of 1992, right around the time Hurricane Andrew was barreling toward Florida, leading to massive evacuations. My wife and I were in Maryland when I got the call that David was dying of late-stage lung cancer, an illness doctors had diagnosed in him about two years after we wrote his life insurance policy. Six months after that phone call, David died with his family and friends at his hospital bedside.

Had it not been for the life insurance, life would have been much different for my sister, who was 33 at the time, and her children. The proceeds from the policy enabled Toni to have some help with the children while she worked full time. She was also able to go back to school and get her master's degree and become a nurse practitioner. Toni eventually remarried and has been blessed with an even larger family now.

I felt this was an important story to tell in this book about the importance of getting life insurance coverage while you can still qualify. The life insurance industry has changed significantly since then. New life insurance contracts are so different that some of them are now considered an asset class.

The New Breed

One of the most intriguing financial assets that is available today, and one that not too many financial advisors even know about, is offered by (drum roll, please) insurance companies. If you were going to build the ideal asset, what features would you include?

Sometimes when I am conducting educational seminars I like to ask the audience, "If you were putting together the perfect financial vehicle, what features would you include?" The responses are interesting. Of course, the *perfect* financial vehicle would have 100 percent liquidity with no risk; provide immediate, double-digit returns; would have no fees; and would have no qualifications. Of course, such a vehicle doesn't exist. There is usually a tradeoff of some kind. For example, a bank CD is safe in that it is insured by the FDIC, but generally offers low interest rates. A stock market investment has the potential for a double-digit return, but comes with a measure of risk.

In a nutshell, here is an overview of some of the features incorporated in the new, index universal life insurance contracts:

- Tax deferred – while it is building up, you pay no taxes and your growth is compounding.
- Potential growth of 1-10 percent each year.
- Tax-free death benefit for heirs
- Not invested in the market
- 100 percent liquidity from day one
- Home health care benefits

You are probably saying, "Alfie, it sounds too good to be true." Am I right? Where's the catch? Well there is a catch. It is life insurance, and you must be healthy enough to qualify. This is not to say that you must be a perfect physical specimen. Insurance companies are accepting most who apply. They understand that many people these days have issues like hypertension (high blood pressure) and diabetes. They accept most of these individuals if their conditions are under control. They will even accept cancer survivors if enough time has elapsed between diagnosis and remission. Index universal life is not a registered security or stock market investment; it doesn't directly participate in any stock or equity investments, or index. The index used is a price index and does not reflect dividends paid on the underlying stocks. Index universal life insurance is subject to limitations, including policy fees and charges, as well as health restrictions and, in some cases, financial underwriting.

Keeping an Open Mind

As I write this, I am on a plane heading to Dallas, Texas, for some additional training. I do this throughout the year. In addition to the academic training I receive at these functions, it also affords me an opportunity to rub shoulders with my professional peers and learn from them. This enables me to keep up with what is happening in the industry and continue to offer my clients the best retirement planning advice possible.

I keep an open mind at these training events. If you don't keep an open mind, you miss out on opportunities. Methods and strategies that worked well 10 years ago may not be as effective today as they once were. A marvelous aspect of a free enterprise society and the free market system is competition. Insurance companies are in competition with banks and Wall Street for retirees' investment dollars. Their product-design people and actuary teams are constantly at the drawing boards, inventing new ways to help retirees and pre-retirees achieve their goals for independent and secure lifestyles once they quit working. Stubbornly clinging to old ideas or refusing to examine new strategies can be harmful to your wealth.

So, dear reader, all I ask of you is to keep an open mind. See for yourself if these new life insurance products may be something that makes sense as part of your overall financial planning picture. You probably nodded your head yes when I said the ideal financial vehicle would contain such features as tax-deferred growth, great earning potential, principal protection, long-term-care benefits, tax-free benefit to heirs, 100 percent liquidity and built-in legacy provisions. But if I had just said "life insurance," you would probably not have even listened. That's understandable. It is human nature to stereotype and shut out new ideas.

My good friend and colleague Sandy Morris held up her cellphone and asked me, "What is this?" I said "It's an iPhone!" "Really?" she replied. "I use it as a computer, GPS, I check on my accounts; I even use it as a flash light. Oh yeah, I do make some calls from it when I'm not texting or emailing!"

The point is, even though it's still a phone, its use has changed over time. It is a mini-computer that contains more data processing capability than the machines that put the first man on the moon. But we still call it a phone, don't we? These new life insurance products are not your grandfather's insurance. We must look at them for what they do, and not what we call them. Like the smartphone, they are tools that serve so many other purposes than the original one for which they were created.

CHAPTER THIRTEEN

What's Keeping YOU up at Night?

During a recent client coaching event, I asked participants to write down on index cards what was keeping them up at night. When I collected them, the top three answers were:

1. ISIS
2. A cyber-attack on the United States power grid
3. The growing national debt.

These are, of course, big problems over which the people in the room had no control. But we could, and did, talk about how national and world affairs can affect our financial affairs, and we discussed how we could plan accordingly.

"Who owns most of our country's debt?" I asked the group. The most popular answer to that question is China. But in reality, the biggest holders of U.S. debt are the Social Security trust funds and other federal government accounts, as well as the Federal Reserve banks. China owns less than 8 percent.

Politics inevitably comes up in these discussions. Which party is better for Wall Street? I tell them that I believe the market is bigger than the presidency.

"Wall Street likes bipartisanship," I said. "It likes checks and balances. Right now we are seeing some volatility because the markets don't like uncertainty. But when things settle down, so should the markets."

But it is also important to diversify. We talk about how people fall short sometimes by investing too heavily in just one or two asset classes.

Another popular topic is gold, because in temperamental times, when the market goes down, you'll see lots of commercials touting this precious metal as a safe haven – a cure for everything. This causes people to wonder if they should change their financial plan and invest more in gold. But the precious metals market is as subject to speculation and volatility as other markets. At one of our workshops, we asked, "Gold: what is it good for?" The answer is that gold is good for jewelry.

Inflation is always a topic of concern. Right now, as I write this, interest rates are low. Oil prices are relatively low. Paying for gasoline at the pump isn't all that painful. People just don't see inflation coming.

But I like to ask, "Have you noticed that cereal boxes are getting smaller?" I've enjoyed Clif Bars for as long as I can remember, and they are definitely getting smaller! Inflation is there, folks; it's just harder to see.

And lastly, not everyone has a pension anymore – those days are over! How do retirees produce income off of their assets during these volatile times? During the *accumulation phase* of life, pre-retirees are contributing to their 401(k)s, IRAs and other retirement accounts. Once you retire, you have entered what I like to call the *harvesting phase*. It is when you enter the harvesting phase of your financial life that you really need a financial coach on your side. It is not uncommon these days for people to be retired for almost as long as they worked. So, it's not so much about what you make; it's about how much you will be able to KEEP of what you make. How much you don't LOSE.

People are losing their hard-earned savings these days in ways they don't even realize. I find that investors are oblivious to all the hidden fees in their accounts, and they fail to recognize the threat inflation has on their future spending. With the odds in your favor for a long life, it's important to have a financial coach who can help create an income plan that you won't outlive. These are the kinds of topics we tackle at our monthly public workshops, quarterly client events and on my weekly "Saving the Investor" radio and TV shows. We coach folks through these challenges and strive to alleviate concerns about how world affairs might affect their financial affairs. We may not be able to solve all of the political problems in the world, but we can help prepare listeners, viewers and clients by focusing on what they can do to prepare for them.

What to Expect When You Visit Us

Please allow me to take this opportunity to tell you what to expect when you come to our office in Fort Myers. It was a bank before we bought it and made it our headquarters. We want everyone to feel very comfortable. We truly try to treat our clients as family. They *are* family.

When you decide to put your life's savings with a firm, you must have total confidence with that firm, and the plan of action you agree upon to provide you with comfort and direction for your retirement.

The first appointment is really just getting to know each other. It is also an opportunity for us to know and understand your dreams and goals. We do not want to, nor can we, work with every person who comes into our office. It must be a good fit.

The second appointment is where we take the information we collected during the first appointment and show you what we have found out. This process is very important, because most of the time, you will find out what you actually own, and what you are paying. We reveal any hidden fees and show you any unnecessary risk you may be taking to obtain the returns on your investments.

In most cases, we are able to reduce that volatility through true diversification in our proprietary portfolios. Also, we are usually able to show you how long your money will last in retirement, and how to make it last throughout your life.

I cannot tell you how many times people come into our office asking me about gold, or what if the dollar devalues, or what will happen if China goes into recession, or ISIS attacks, or some other major concern. We use computer programs the U.S. government used in the 2008 financial crisis to show different scenarios and how your portfolio might perform during times of crisis. They are worth a look-see! We try to look at the total picture and craft for you a sound retirement plan with which you can be comfortable and in which you can have confidence.

I am not saying that you will not experience volatility, but what I am saying is you will not be taking *unnecessary* risk in order to produce returns in your portfolio. Also, you will not go into panic mode like the average investor does when the market enters a downturn.

A good financial coach helps you take the emotion out of investing by creating a customized retirement income plan. A plan that will keep you comfortably in the fairway and well away from the traps and hazards that could otherwise ensnare you once you enter what I sincerely hope will prove to be the most enjoyable years of your life.

About the Author

A lfie Tounjian is president and founder of Advantage Retirement Group, a financial advisory firm with offices in several Florida cities and one in Eldersburg, Maryland. The firm's headquarters is in Fort Myers, Florida, where Alfie and his wife, Tommie, live and work. Alfie has attained the CERTIFIED FINANCIAL PLANNER™ designation, having become a CFP® professional through American College of Financial Services. He has also earned the Registered Financial Consultant (RFC®) designation and passed the Series 65 securities examination, which makes him a fiduciary. He is also licensed as a life/health/annuity insurance agent.

Alfie shares his financial planning philosophy on his popular radio and television show, "Saving the Investor." He began his career in the financial services profession in 1983 when, after college, he relocated to Maryland and opened his first office.

Alfie prefers "coaching" rather than managing his clients, helping them take advantage of proprietary programs and strategies designed to help grow and preserve their financial assets. His techniques are particularly appealing to people who would rather spend time enjoying their lives and retirement, confident in the knowledge that they have a retirement income strategy customized to their needs and goals without their constant attention.

Alfie and his family attend Next Level Church in Fort Myers. He enjoys playing golf on the challenging courses of south Florida and relaxing on his boat when he can on the beautiful waters of the Gulf.

Alfie's Story

Alfie's mother, Sandy Glass, came from a large family. She had two brothers and three sisters and she was the second youngest of the bunch. She was reared in Henderson, Kentucky. Her father was a hard worker and her mother stayed at home to care of the family.

"Mom lost her parents at the tender age of 11," Alfie said. "My grandfather died of lung disease her mother from a gall bladder ailment. So my mom was raised by her older sister, my Aunt Pat, who had just finished nursing school and now found herself in a position of having to work to take care of her two younger siblings."

"My mom and her younger brother were put in a tough spot at a young age," he explains. "Between Aunt Pat, Aunt Judy and Uncle Buddy, they did the best they could to take turns of caring for my mom and Uncle Rich."

Alfie said his grandmother and grandfather did not have life insurance, which would have helped with the raising of the young children, a fact that motivated him professionally when he became an adult. When his mother was 14, she moved from Kentucky and went to live with her brother, Buddy, and his wife in New York. Buddy had a good job, working for IBM.

"My mother was a beautiful woman who, when she was young, looked much older than her age," Alfie said. "She got some modeling jobs in New York, and while she was there, she met my dad. They married when my mother was 15 and moved to California, where his people are from. My sister, Antoinette Marie (Toni) Tounjian was brought into the world when my mother was only 16. Seventeen months later, I was born."

Alfie says he really doesn't remember much about his father. He and his mother were divorced when Alfie was 5. His father was a Teamster truck driver, which meant he wasn't home very much. Sandy and the children moved to Miami Beach, Florida, in 1966 to be with her older sister, Pat. He said his mother worked as a waitress trying to make ends meet. Those years were hard times for the young family.

Early Days with Mother

"My sister and I remember the different apartments we lived in," Alfie recounted. "There were times when we lost our electricity because Mom didn't have the money to pay the bill. But that is why Toni and I have such a tight relationship – because of the hard times all three of us had to endure. We went to several different schools because we moved around a lot. At least we got to meet new people each year."

It was when Alfie was in the fourth grade that his mother had to make the hardest decision of her life – sending him and Toni to Florida Methodist Children's Home.

"It was a difficult time for all of us, but it was also the right choice," Alfie explained. "The children's home gave my sister and me structure. We lived in the same group home with 16 other kids. Toni was always there for me. The home had all the kids doing their chores every day. Saturdays, we would get to sleep a little later in the morning. Then on Sunday, there was church with a great early dinner afterwards."

That year was also part of a big transition for Alfie and Toni as it was the year their father died of lung cancer.

"My sister and I flew out to California to visit with Dad at his place just before he died," Alfie said. "After Dad's death, life became more normal because Mom started receiving his Social Security for Toni and me. We were able to reunite as a family and move into a nicer apartment. Mom was able to move up the ranks with a major department store. She managed the whole shoe department."

"We always knew our mother loved us more than anything in the world," Alfie said. "She taught us compassion and the value of hard work. I once asked Mom if she wished she had had us later in life and, without hesitation, she said no. We always knew that what Mom did was for our protection – to give us something better until she was able to work it out."

Alfie acknowledges that both he and Toni were blessed to have such an amazing, giving and sharing person in their mother. "Mom taught me never to give up, and to have faith to get you through hard times."

"My older sister, Toni, helped my mom a lot with the cooking because Mom worked late hours," said Alfie. "To this day, I have not eaten Hamburger Helper since 1976."

Sandy embraces an almost-grown Alfie in 1980 as he prepares for his senior prom.

Teenage Years

Due to Sandy's long hours spent working trying to provide for her children, Alfie admits he may have had "too much freedom" as he transitioned into adolescence.

"You could say I had too much time on my hands," Alfie said. "When I was in seventh grade, we moved from Bradenton to Temple Terrace, Florida. Unfortunately, my first choice of friends was the bad kids in the neighborhood. Needless to say, 'Birds of a feather flock together.' So I was a handful for my poor mom between the seventh and eighth grades.

"But then something changed my life in 1976 that helped me see things differently. Believe it or not, it was the movie "Rocky," which came out when I was about 13 or 14 years old. It just struck a chord so strong with me that it changed me both mentally and physically. I began working out, studying hard, and hanging with a new group of uplifting kids. I have tried to let Sylvester Stallone know how he changed my life, but without success. I will keep trying."

Introduction to Amway

"I remember the day I was introduced to Amway," recalls Alfie. "I had just graduated from high school, and I still had my job selling shoes at Florsheim Thayer McNeil, an upper-end shoe store in Tampa. It was a great job for a kid in high school finding his way in life. An elderly couple came into the store one night. They were probably only in their mid-60s, but I was only 19, and to me anyone over 40 was elderly. Their names were Tom and Gerry. Yes... those were their real names."

"I'll never forget that night," continued Alfie. "I asked them if I could help them with anything, and they started a conversation with me. One of the questions was if I ever thought about working for myself. Even though I was only 19, believe it or not, I was always a big thinker. I said, 'Yes, I have.'"

"I asked them what they did, and they told me they were in the import and export business," Alfie said. "I thought that was intriguing, so I asked them what they imported and exported. That's when the sales pitch began."

"They said that it was many things, and that they were looking to expand in this area and would I like to learn about their business," Alfie said. "What would any 19-year-old do who was searching for something but really did not know what it was they were searching for? So I said sure."

Alfie remembers the couple was good. They set up the appointment for a week later – enough time to get him really excited. The appointment was to be in their home in the evening.

"If you know me, you know I wanted to know everything right then – not a week from now, but I held it together until the evening of the appointment," said Alfie. "In the meantime, I was in a very good mood because someone had thought enough about me to offer me something that seemed to be an awesome opportunity."

"A few days before the appointment, I told a sales associate at the shoe store about Tom and Gerry, our conversation, and the upcoming meeting," said Alfie. "He immediately said, 'Amway.' And, of course, he was negative. His words didn't really affect me one way. He tried to explain multi-level marketing, but I didn't get it."

"When the night of the big meeting came, I walked into their small, older home in Tampa, not knowing what to expect," Alfie remembers. "We had dinner and then started talking about their import/export business. Tom started drawing circles on paper. 'This is you,' he said. Then he drew six more circles. 'These are your friends or people you meet.' All I remember was the circles kept coming and coming."

"Then he said, 'if you help people get what they want, then you will get what you want.'"

"They asked me if I could think of what I used over and over again," Alfie said. "I said toilet paper. He said, 'what about soap?' I said yes. That's when he told me that what he was talking about here was Amway."

"I have to say that I was disappointed," Alfie related. "Mainly because of the negative comments my sales associate had expressed. But after I got over my disappointment, I sat with Tom and Gerry and we talked for a long time about the history of the company and the kind of people who were involved with it. I think it was $50 to get started with a sales number and some products. The circles made it seem so easy on paper. But it didn't quite turn out quite that way."

Alfie says, "I was fortunate enough to be sponsored by someone that was already pretty high up, and knew the big Amway players. That was good and bad. I had a lot of high expectations for a young 19-year-old who had no money and big dreams. These big Amway superstars would introduce me as the up-and-coming super kid. Everyone seemed to have a Cadillac. And the really big ones traveled in their own Motorhomes."

Alfie says that Amway was a great introduction to being an entrepreneur.

"I always thought big, but these people had **huge** dreams and goals that dwarfed mine," says Alfie. "I think the problem most of us have is not having a clear-cut goal in life. That applies to the way people plan for retirement, too."

Alfie recalls his excitement when he contemplated the success that was just around the corner with his new opportunity.

"As previously mentioned, I was introduced to some of the big people that had already had success in the business, so it was easy to get excited about my new opportunity that I was about to have."

It may have been that Alfie's exposure to the higher-ups of Amway gave him eyes that were bigger than his stomach, so to speak.

"Like my stepdad, Jack, would say, 'the only time you start on top is when you're digging a hole,'" said Alfie. "That is what happened to me in the Amway business. Because of all the successful people I was hanging around, I thought it would naturally follow that I would have that success too. But my success didn't come. It was not for lack of trying. I remember my sponsor telling me that I needed to go to all the functions, and success would follow. I told him, 'I don't have the money to go.' His response I will never forget: 'If you want to be a success, you have to do what other people are not willing to do.'"

"So I went to all the events to hear speakers and learn about how to grow your business," Alfie said. "The best part was going to Denny's for breakfast after the meetings where we would talk and dream with each other about our 'prosperity' until midnight."

The young Alfie took his sponsor's advice about "doing what others weren't willing to do" to heart, pushing himself to do whatever it took to be a reliable go-getter.

"One time I asked my Aunt Pat for help," Alfie said. "Could I use her car (she was a nurse) to attend a meeting in Orlando? She said yes, but she needed it in the morning to drive to work. I said no problem and I would be home around midnight. After the meeting, around 10 of us met at Denny's and talked until almost 1 a.m. I knew I had to get that car back, so I hit the road in the wee hours. I was so tired, but I had to keep driving. I put my face out of the window to wake me up. I must have done that 20 times or more. I pulled over at a rest area and splashed water on my face. It was the worst drive of my life. By the time I rolled into the driveway, the sun was coming up. But I did get the car back in time for Aunt Pat to drive it to work. I kept my promise."

Alfie continued, "To this day, I talk to my son, Devon, who, along with my nephew David Pavey, is now working with us, and tell them that their word is their bond. Clients are trusting me and my team with their life's savings. They must have confidence in your word."

"Another lesson my short time in Amway taught me is that people with whom you associate determine your attitude," Alfie pointed out. "It is not easy to stay positive when we have 24-hour news stations and the internet pumping out negative information telling all the bad news. But it is easier if you surround yourself with people you love and admire. The speakers at Amway events were very motivating. They were all about the American Dream. Their mantra was 'work for yourself and hang around with leaders if you want to become one.'"

"The last, and most important lesson I learned from my Amway experience was way back in 1981," recounted Alfie. "I was in an event in Atlanta with around 15,000 people. This was a three-day event that ended on Sunday morning with a church service. The speaker was a well-known preacher. I always believed in God, but did not go to church too often at that point. I was listening to the preacher, and toward the end of the sermon, he said that if anyone wanted to accept the Lord as their savior, they should just come up front. I saw people walking toward the front, so I joined in. Then it happened. I was standing there and he was saying some words, and I felt a rush go through my body that I had never felt before. Later on, I was told it was Holy Spirit."

"So, although I was not a success in Amway," said Alfie. "Amway was a success with me."

A Career Change for Sandy

Around the time Alfie was picking up invaluable entrepreneurial experience with Amway, Sandy had a career change. She was tired of retail and, in 1981, saw a newspaper advertisement for insurance agents.

"I was in school and working full time," said Alfie. "This was a whole new world for my mother. I remember helping her study for her insurance test. She passed with flying colors and started her insurance career with health insurance, Medicare supplement policies and life insurance."

Alfie said she did so well in her new job that it created an opportunity for him to get into the insurance industry two years later. Shortly after that, Sandy married Alfie's stepfather, Jack Glass.

Alfie said his mother enjoyed helping her clients and was a great listener.

"Her clients loved her," he said. "She had to leave the business due to health reasons, so I decided I would try it. That was 1983 and I was 21 years old. My fear was that no one would want to do business with a 21-year-old. But a mentor, and a veteran of the business, told me people want to do business with people they like and relate to. He also told me I had better know my products inside and out. To this day I take pride in knowing everything I know about what we offer – whether it is our services, investments, insurance or legacy planning."

Life Lessons Learned

"Growing up without a lot of money may have been difficult at times, but it taught me a lot about life that I would never have learned otherwise," said Alfie. "It gave me the work ethic I needed and the strength of character I needed to succeed in the business world."

Alfie says that one of the greatest sources of satisfaction he has in his work is meeting new clients from so many different walks of life. When he first started in the financial services business in 1983, there was no internet. There were also no 24-hour news channels. Investing was simpler in those days, Alfie says.

"These days, it requires much more discipline because we live in an age of information overload," Alfie said. "We are inundated with infomercials, news alerts, phone alerts, continuous information to make us feel uneasy about the future."

Alfie said this is why he calls his radio and television show "Saving the Investor."

"My mission is to share my knowledge and experience and spread a positive note to people, letting them know there are steps they can take and things they can do to grow and safeguard their money, and have the retirement they have always wanted," Alfie explained.

What we experience in our early life shapes us later on. Alfie's insistence on his son and nephew learning the value of keeping promises came from an experience he had when he was young that impressed upon him a very important life lesson.

"Growing up, I was determined to always do anything I told people I was going to do," says Alfie. "When I was 9 years old, living with my Aunt Pat, another of my mother's sisters called to talk to Mom. She was out, and so my Aunt Judy asked me what I wanted for Christmas. I told her I wanted a new bicycle. She asked me what kind. I told her a Schwinn Varsity. She asked me what color. I told her green."

"I will get you that bike for Christmas," she promised.

"I was so excited," said Alfie. "I just knew that I would get that bike. Aunt Judy had a heart of gold. She never married and grew up in Kentucky, working in a factory her whole life. She only had a sixth grade education, but she was a hard worker and did not depend on anyone but herself. Christmas came, but my bike did not. I later found out that my Aunt Judy liked her Busch Beer, and probably meant it at the time, but quickly forgot her promise."

"I tell you this story because I never forgot how disappointing a broken promise can be," said Alfie. "I never want to say what I cannot do."

"I also learned the hard way the value of planning," said Alfie. "My mother's parents had no plan in place to protect their family when they passed away at a young age. Had they had one, life would have been much better for Mom. As it was, she really never had a childhood."

Alfie says that this is why one of his main concerns in financial planning is continuation of income for the spouse left behind.

"I dive into what will be the income for the surviving spouse," he says. "We want to create a plan that addresses as many contingencies as possible."

These are only a few of the experiences that have shaped Alfie, both personally and professionally. Alfie says being a CERTIFIED FINANCIAL PLANNER™ professional is a big responsibility because people who come to his office and decide to do business with him trust him with their life's savings. Instead of presenting cookie-cutter plans and products, Alfie – as a CFP® professional and fiduciary – takes on the responsibility of helping the people who put their trust in him use those life's savings to craft a strategy tailored to their personal goals, dreams and needs.

"That is a responsibility I can never take lightly," Alfie said.

Acknowledgements

I want to thank my wife, Tommie, for being my rock and best friend. If it was not for her, I know I would not be where I am today! We are an amazing team! It's been a great 30 years and I'm looking forward to the next.

My son, Devon, makes me proud. He is going to college, and is working here at our office, learning the business.

I want my mom, Sandy, to know that Toni and I are blessed to have you as our mom. You always loved us, and are the most caring person I know.

While writing this book, I remember stories from my early years that help shape me. My sister, Toni, has always been there for the family. Life wasn't always easy for us, but we always had each other. And now I have the privilege to mentor your son, David Pavey. Love you, sis.

Mary Thompson worked very hard with me on this book. I most likely would have put it off for many years if Mary had not been there to push me to dig deeper, and keep reminding me that people really do want to know my story. Thank you for all your hard work with this endeavor.

I extend my gratitude to Tom Bowen, a true professional who helped me through the hard parts, made valuable structural and content suggestions and kept me going when the press of other business was in the way. I treasure your friendship and immense value as a writing coach.

Pastor John Antonucci has been not just a great friend, but he has given me the confidence to try things that I never imagined I could do. I now enjoy doing the "Saving the Investor" radio hour of power, and the TV show that has changed me immeasurably. He is also a great, Godly man.

Last but not least, I thank my Lord, Jesus Christ, for giving me this amazing life. My family and I are so grateful for the opportunity to touch the lives of so many people who have become a big part of our lives.

Cheers and Blessings!
~Alfie

The author enjoys a day with family, from left: Alfie's wife, Tommie; Alfie; niece-in-law, Laura; mother, Sandy; nephew, David; great-nephew, Blake; and sister, Toni.

From left, Devon, Simona, Alfie and Tommie relax, boating together.

More than my mother, I dedicate this to a woman who
always shared more laughter than tears.

Made in the USA
Columbia, SC
24 June 2021